Advance Praise

We don't see nearly enough books about friendship, but *Girl, Unpack That!* by Lisa Najarian fills that gap beautifully. Inspired by a girls' weekend getaway, Lisa takes an honest look at the emotional weight women carry and the power of sharing it. She even offers a practical way to build stronger, more meaningful friendships through her BAGS framework: Bonding, Awareness, Guidance, and Sisterhood.

This book felt especially personal to me. I've stayed close with a group of high school girlfriends, and we reunite every year. There's something powerful in those gatherings, and this book captures that spirit while encouraging us to go even deeper.

Girl, Unpack That! is the kind of read that makes you want to reach out to a friend and remind her she's not alone.

—Denise LeClaire Cobb
Former CNN Anchor
Philanthropist

Lisa Najarian sums up female friendship as well as I've ever heard it explained. This is the perfect book for the woman in your life who carries the weight of the world on her shoulders and needs to be reminded that she's not alone. I have four daughters who are strong women and are constant reminders to me that I am never alone. Each one of my girls will love this book as much as I have.

—Stacey Cooper
Supermodel, Mrs. Globe 2001
Lifestyle Entrepreneur

Lisa (Loopie) Najarian's story is heartwarming and inspiring, honest and fun. Definitely motivates you to want to call up a girlfriend and keep in touch with your friends more.

—Ally Hilfiger
Artist, Author, Lyme Advocate

Girl, Unpack That! is a blueprint for women ready to set down what they've carried in silence, tell the truth to the friends who love them, and rediscover themselves in the safety of sisterhood. Lisa Najarian shares her journey from a childhood spent performing for her mother's approval to a life built on the kind of friendship that requires no performance at all. Through humor, vulnerability, and hard-earned wisdom, *Girl, Unpack That!* reminds us how much we still need each other, and how rarely we admit it.

—David Perozzi
Former ABC News Executive Producer

Girl, Unpack That! touches on loss, identity, addiction, illness, and self-worth without ever feeling heavy-handed. Instead, each page feels intimate and real. Lisa's journey, in particular, anchors the entire book with emotional depth. Raw, relatable, and touching, this book shines.

—Carrie Sisson
Co-Founder of Primal Kitchen
Author and Women's Motivational Speaker

Girl, Unpack That!

The Trip That Changed Me and the Framework That Can Change You

LISA NAJARIAN

GIRL, UNPACK THAT!
The Trip That Changed Me and the Framework That Can Change You

For permissions requests, podcast interviews, speaking inquiries, and bulk order purchase options, email yougogirlcommunity@gmail.com.
You Go Girl
PO Box 595
Willernie, MN 55090
You-Go-Girl.com

ISBN: 979-8-9955851-0-7

In collaboration with Kathy Haskins
Edited by Lori Lynn Enterprises
Photography by Kristie Anderson and Dominique Najarian
Designed by Transcendent Publishing

DISCLAIMER: This is a work of creative nonfiction based on the author's personal story, but other character names, places, and incidents are either the product of the author's imagination or are used fictitiously. Any resemblance to actual persons, living or dead (other than the author and her family), or specific events is entirely coincidental and unintentional.

"Since I was young, I have always known this: Life damages us, every one. We can't escape that damage. But now, I am also learning this: We can be mended. We mend each other."

—*Veronica Roth*

For Edna, my mom, who showed me at a young age that change is the only thing that's certain. Your discontent had me forever meeting and leaving friends, teaching me to recognize happiness through sadness and to say hello and goodbye as though both were the price of surviving … and you were right.

Contents

Foreword

Let me tell you something about Lisa Najarian. That woman will plan the hell out of a girls' trip, and once you're there, she will greet you with the warmest hug and listen with all her heart.

I wasn't on the original trip she took with her oldest friends that served as the inspiration for this book, but I know Lisa, which means I can tell you exactly how it went. She was *all in*. One thousand percent!

She's the one who wraps the trip in a big red bow. Customized playlists. Gifts on the pillows. A charcuterie board worthy of a Michelin star. She handles every detail nobody else wants to think about, and she still walks in acting like she hadn't spent endless hours planning the whole thing. It's one of my favorite things about her.

She thinks of everything, and she does it because that is genuinely how Lisa loves people ... or perhaps ... it's something deeper.

So when she called me and said she was writing a book about girlfriendship, I smiled. I wasn't even a little surprised. I thought, *Finally!* I'd been waiting for her to put her story down on paper.

Of course she found a way to take what happened on her trip and bottle that magic so she could hand it to other women. That is so completely, utterly, perfectly Lisa. She cannot have a meaningful experience without immediately wanting to share it with everyone she cares about.

What I didn't expect was how much I needed to read it.

At some point, life, kids, parents, and work get in the way of the present, and most of us just get used to carrying things alone. Some of us learn to keep the real stuff private and share only what dresses up our social media accounts.

We get good at saying "I'm fine" before the question is even finished. We build beautiful, busy lives and fill them with noise and notifications. We text. We post. We like each other's pics and drop heart emojis and "likes" to give the illusion that we're paying attention, but when do we ever just pick up the phone? There's an abundance of contact but a lack of connection.

And we tell ourselves that counts?

It doesn't count. Not really. And deep down, most of us already know this. We just haven't said it out loud because we feel like we don't have the time to deal with it.

But time is precious. So are you. So am I. So are those few really good friends we can actually go deep with.

What would happen if, even for one night, we were completely honest with ourselves … and with each other?

What you are holding right now is proof of what can happen when we unpack our emotional baggage together. It is the story of five women who thought they were going on vacation and instead stumbled into the most honest conversations of their lives. Really close friends who had known each other for decades but still had secrets they had never spoken out loud. Strong, capable, accomplished women who'd pretended the weight of their secrets wasn't heavy.

Sound familiar?

This book invites you to take a sincere look at what you've been dragging around—the grief, the anger, the shame, the dream you set down so quietly nobody even noticed, the thing you never said to the person you should have said it to—and be willing to share the load with someone you trust.

Women have always been each other's greatest resource. Long before there were therapists or self-help sections or wellness podcasts, there were women gathered around fires and kitchen tables and back porches, telling the truth. Holding each other up. Reminding each other who they were when the world had done its best to make them forget.

Lisa gets this. She's been through enough to know—really know—and it shows in how she shows up for people. Something about her makes the laughter come easy, and once that happens, the harder stuff tends to follow. She built that space at a beach house in California, and while the friends in these pages are shaped by imagination, every emotion in this book is completely real.

So pull up a chair. Put on your cozies. Pour yourself something good and let these pages remind you that you have more people in your corner than you realize.

You're not alone. Not too broken, too busy, too proud, or too private. You're just a woman with a heavy bag filled with responsibility and a story worth telling.

Girl, Unpack That! promises to inspire you to take time to reach out and reconnect.

Our bags have been heavy long enough.

—Jo LaMarca Mathisen
Daytime Emmy Award–Winning Producer
Executive Producer, *The M Factor Film Series*
Former Executive Producer, NBC/Today's 4th hour,
Kathie Lee & Hoda and *Hoda & Jenna*

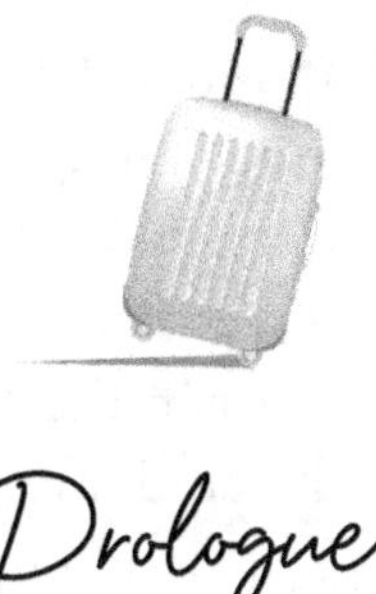

Prologue

M y phone rang. It was a 916 area code. I knew it must be Mary, my mom's nurse.

"Hello?"

"Hi Lisa, it's Mary. I just got to your mom's house. I'm here with her now, and it's not good."

My heart started to pound. My mom had never been in the best of health. She'd been a poor eater most of her life. She was a two-pack-a-day cigarette smoker, and she was overweight. Breast cancer had made its rounds with her in the last decade, and she was no spring chicken at eighty-three.

I was on Central Time and Mary was on Pacific, so it was early for her (seven a.m.) when she called. I had been sitting at my desk in my cozy office, staring out the window at our front yard. Outside, the ground was trying to sparkle with a diamond-like white layer of snow, but the sky was too gray to give off any reflection.

My younger years were spent in Sacramento, California, where spring always promised temperate weather, blooming flowers, and the freedom to be outside comfortably. But for the past thirty-plus years, I'd lived either on the East Coast or in the Midwest. You'd think I would've adjusted to the cold after all these years, right? Nope. That morning, I desperately wished for those Sacramento spring days, daydreaming of that sunshine I love.

The call from Mary jolted me back to reality. "Not good, like, get-on-a-plane not good?" I asked.

"Yes, I think that's the best idea. It looks as though she's had a stroke. She's immobile and can't speak."

I asked her to put the phone up to Mom's ear. I heard a gurgle—that damn "death rattle" people talk about when someone is about to die.

In a crackly voice, I tried to console her. "Hang on, Mom, I'm on my way. I'll be there soon!"

I hung up and immediately dialed my husband, Pete. Isn't it funny how you can hold it together for so long, but when you need to speak to someone in this type of situation—someone you know loves and cares for you—you instantly lose it? My tears started to flow as I anticipated Pete answering the phone.

Two rings later, I heard, "Hi!"

"I need you to get me a ticket to go out to Mom because today is going to be her last."

"Hey, what happened? Are you okay?"

Sniffling and trying to clear my throat, I said, "She had a stroke last night. I need to be there for her in the last moments of her life. No one ever wants to die the way she is dying. I can, at least, be by her side in the end."

"I'm on it," he said.

I ran upstairs, walked into my closet, and opened one of the cabinet doors. I pulled down my signature pink suitcase from the top shelf. I stood there, looking around, trying to decide what I needed to visit my mother for the last time in my life. But nothing in there—no fancy shoes or brand-name clothes—could take away the empty feeling I had.

Realizing it didn't really matter what I brought, I packed the basics and left for the airport. Security was light, so I got to my gate quickly, walked down the jet bridge to board the plane, and noticed Pete had graciously put me in first class. *I love that man!*

By eight thirty that evening, I was sitting outside of my mom's ugly salmon-colored mobile home in my rented truck, gathering my thoughts.

"This is it, isn't it?" I said out loud to myself.

I had a lump in my throat the size of a golf ball, and I was ready to burst into tears, but I didn't want to be a mess when I got in there. I needed to be strong for her. The doll that she'd carried around all those years had returned to be by her side.

This is the very last day I will ever see my mom. I will not hear her voice. I will not feel her touch. I will not look into her eyes—ever again.

It was a crushing thought.

I chose to leave all of my judgment, criticism, and pain in that stupid rented truck and decided to offer her grace for the last time in our lives. A little too little and a little too late, but I would give her my best.

Blinking back tears, I thought, *This is truly the end.*

I got out of the truck and walked into her home. That stale scent of her cigarettes almost knocked me over, but I went straight to Mom's room as quickly as I could. John, her boyfriend, and my half-brother, Bill, were sitting close to her.

Mom was lying on her left side, facing us, near the edge of her bed. A faded yellow sheet and a tan fleece blanket covered her, making her look frail. Her eyes were open, but she wasn't really there.

Her labored breathing was so much worse in person than over the phone. That awful gurgle filled the room, making her seem like a monster—like a character in a scary movie. To this day, that sound, mingled with the stale, sickly-sweet smell of her breath, continues to haunt me.

I wanted to play Elvis's "Peace in the Valley" for her, knowing it was what she would have wanted, but I hesitated, scared I might miss her final moments.

Instead, I sat on the edge of her bed, took her hands in mine, and started talking to her, not knowing if she could hear or understand me.

"I'm here now, Mom. I'm so sorry you have to go through this. I love you. You can go if you want—it's okay."

Her breathing became irregular, stopping and starting again. I felt utterly helpless, caught between wanting her to stay and wishing for her suffering to end.

Bill sat behind me on a chair in the corner. I searched his face. "I don't know what to do! What should I do?" I sobbed, my panic rising. Bill had tears in his eyes, but he couldn't find the words to answer me.

I turned back as Mom took her last breath, her hands still in mine. The stillness that followed was both eerie and peaceful.

Later, as we waited for the crematory to pick up her body, questions started flooding my mind. I couldn't help but wonder how on earth I made it to her in time. We had only fifteen minutes together. *Was it because Pete put me in first class? What if I had been at the back of the plane? Would I have missed her? Was she waiting for me to get there? Did she really listen when I told her on the phone hours before, "Hang on, I'm on my way"?*

I'd always made the effort to be there for Edna London, my mother. It had been a long, difficult road, but I'd shown up for her. Even when it wasn't easy. And I'd given her grace in her last moments. That seemed to allow me to have no regrets.

At least, that's what I told myself.

A Note from the Author

One week after my mom died, I found myself in yet another airport. The effort of packing up my mom's life and giving it all away had left me physically exhausted and emotionally numb. But I wasn't headed home to Minnesota. Instead, I was headed to Santa Barbara for a long-planned girlfriends' trip with four of my closest friends.

I should have canceled. I was in no shape to be good company. But grief is a strange thing—it doesn't follow logic or etiquette. And somewhere deep down, I knew I needed this. I needed to not think about my mother. I needed to not think about death. I needed to laugh and cook and play and pretend—just for a few days. I needed to remember that life could still be normal.

Since we were twelve years old, these girls had been my foundation, my ride-or-die crew, my chosen family. Rachel, Maya, Leah, and Amber. We knew the good, the bad, and the ugly about each other. They'd been there through everything—all the moves, all the chaos of my childhood with Edna. They knew Edna very well, but I didn't want to talk about her or her death. Not this weekend. This weekend was about fun with my girlfriends, not focusing on my feelings.

A short flight later, I arrived in Santa Barbara carrying two things: one well-loved suitcase filled with clothes and travel-sized toiletries, and one invisible carry-on stuffed with decades of emotional baggage I had no intention of unpacking.

I was the strong one. The overachiever. The planner who runs a tight ship. The woman who could walk into any room and instantly make friends. That's how I'd survived my chaotic childhood—by being good, being perfect, being whatever people needed me to be. On this trip, my friends needed Fun Lisa. Not Grieving Lisa. Not Angry Lisa. Not the Lisa who was carrying around a lifetime of hurt from a mother who could never quite show up for her.

So I zipped it all up tight and walked toward baggage claim, ready to play the part.

We thought we were just getting together to catch up on each other's lives and have some fun.

We had no idea something powerful was about to happen.

We didn't know that one woman's story—a shocking truth told over lunch in Ojai—would crack us all open. That in a single weekend, we'd all be finally naming the things we'd been carrying in silence for decades. The secrets. The shame. The regret. The anger. The grief. All of it, packed down and hauled around like dead weight for years.

I wasn't the only one carrying baggage that weekend.

But I didn't know that yet.

One

onths before my mom passed, I was missing my oldest friends, so I reached out to them and told them I wanted to plan a girls' trip for all of us. Were they in? All four girls answered with a resounding "YES!"

I'm a planner. An organizer. When I focus on something like this, it consumes me—but in the best way.

I spent weeks planning this trip. I found the cutest Airbnb on Miramar Beach in Santa Barbara overlooking the Pacific Ocean, and I booked it immediately. It had a huge kitchen with extra counter space—essential for the kind of cooking I had planned. I love to cook, especially for others, so I mapped out a full menu and made my shopping list.

All of my memories with these girls were filled with music, so I spent hours reminiscing as I crafted the perfect "Santa Barbara Babes" Spotify playlist—AC/DC, Van Halen, Billy Squier, The Cars, The Greg Kihn Band, George Thorogood, John Cougar Mellencamp. Songs that would take us right back to high school. After a few cocktails, I knew we'd be dancing like we were in the movie *Flashdance*.

In all my planning and researching, I stumbled across some adorable coffee cups on social media. I am a sucker for those ads. You could customize what each woman looked like from the back—no faces, just the backs of five women sitting arm in arm on a dock by the water.

This is the sweetest, most perfect gift for the girls, I thought.

I carefully selected each detail: Rachel's short brown hair, Maya's long blonde waves, Leah's shoulder-length light-brown hair, Amber's mousy-brown shoulder-length cut, and my curly blonde hair. It looked just like us.

I also found bracelets with different charms you could buy. I found the perfect charm and added five of them to the cart.

I rounded out the package with lip and eye masks and clicked "buy." These gifts would include heartfelt cards for each of them. I couldn't wait to give them their gifts.

When I landed in Santa Barbara, I went straight to pick up the black Jeep Wrangler Unlimited I'd reserved. The rental guy helped me get the top off right there in the lot. It would be a tight fit for our luggage on the way to and from the airport, but the Jeep would be perfect for our sunny California weekend.

I had a couple of hours before the girls' flights arrived, so I headed to Whole Foods. I grabbed the basics: eggs, bread, and some condiments. Then I added the ingredients for the dish I'd been planning: fresh zucchini, the good Parmesan in a wedge, pine nuts, and asparagus. And can you even have a party without a charcuterie board? For dessert, I picked up some gelato. There was a store near the Airbnb that made artisan chocolates. No way was I going to miss that stop!

I moved on to our assorted drinks. Coffee and hot tea for the mornings. I picked up some wine and that trusty Patrón Silver tequila, then paused. Amber had mentioned she wasn't drinking anymore. I grabbed some sparkling water, fresh-squeezed lemonade, cranberry juice, and a few bottles of kombucha.

I had so many bags in tow that the handles were indenting my arms. I piled them into the Jeep and headed down the 101 to our beach house.

So, this is what it's like to live on the Pacific Ocean, I thought as I arrived. The sun was golden without any clouds to dim the light. I could taste and smell the salt from the ocean spray and knew this was the perfect place to share the weekend with the girls. The view helped me focus on something other than my grief.

I had Pete pack a box of items from home and ship it to me—my hand-crank zucchini noodle spiralizer, the good knives, and two jars of the homemade pesto I'd made from my garden basil. The Airbnb kitchen would have the basics, but I wanted my own tools. My comfort.

He added the personalized coffee cups and other stuff I had ordered and thankfully remembered to pack my old yearbooks from middle school and high school that I had laid aside. I couldn't wait to look them over as a group. The last item in the box was my bright orange Bop Bluetooth speaker—a little speaker with a huge sound.

Once the groceries were put away, I laid out the wrapped coffee cups, lip and eye masks, and cards on each pillow in the bedrooms. I wanted them to know how special they were to me.

Now it was time to race back to the airport to pick up my four besties. I kept thinking, *This weekend together is going to be so great!*

As I sat in the Jeep's passenger seat with the door wide open and watched people stream through the automatic doors, my chest tightened with anticipation. How long had it been since we were all together? Life had gotten so busy, and somewhere along the way, our group texts had gone quiet, and our phone calls had become less frequent.

But we were here now. That's what mattered.

Rachel came through first. Her brown hair had grown back in soft wisps—not quite as long as she used to wear it, but it looked great on her. She'd lost weight, but she still moved with that same purposeful energy I remembered from high school when she'd stride down the hallways like she owned the place.

I jumped out and sprinted toward her.

"Rach!"

"Lisa!" She dropped her bag and pulled me into a tight hug. When she let go, I could see the exhaustion around her eyes, but also something else—relief, maybe. "God, I needed this weekend. If I have to explain my insurance coverage to one more billing department, I'm gonna lose my mind."

"At least you're retired now. No more board meetings, no more middle schoolers throwing food in the cafeteria—"

"Don't remind me about the food fights. I still have PTSD." She laughed, and I heard that big, generous sound I'd missed so much. "Where are the others?"

"Should be coming any minute. How was your flight?"

"Easy. Slept through most of it, which is a miracle."

Before I could respond, I heard a squeal behind me.

"LADIES!"

Maya and Leah burst through the doors together, both talking at once. Maya's long blonde hair was pulled back in a messy bun, and she wore yoga pants and an oversized sweatshirt that read: Be nice. One day I might be your nurse. Leah, on the other hand, looked like she'd stepped out of a magazine—perfectly fitted jeans, a cream-colored cashmere sweater, and caramel-colored ankle boots. Not a hair out of place.

The four of us collided in a group hug, none of us listening to what anyone else was saying because we were all talking at once.

"—can't believe we're actually here—"

"—flight was delayed in Denver for like two hours—"

"—Rachel, your hair looks great!"

"—and did you see that guy with the ferret? An actual ferret on the plane—"

"—I'm starving, when do we eat—"

Finding a tiny lull in all the excitement, I asked, "You two flew together?"

"Last-minute thing," Maya said. "Leah texted me two days ago asking if I wanted to switch my flight."

"I hate flying alone," Leah admitted. "Plus, this way we could split an Uber to the airport so I could vent about my latest client who wants to wallpaper her ceiling. Her ceiling, you guys."

"That's not even the worst part," Maya jumped in. "She showed me pictures. It's like floral explosion meets Victorian funeral parlor."

"I tried to talk her out of it," Leah said. "I showed her Pinterest boards. I gave her options. She said, and I quote,

'I want people to feel something when they walk into my bedroom.'"

"Nausea," Rachel deadpanned. "They'll feel nausea."

Leah threw up her hands. "Exactly!"

"Where's Amber?" I asked, looking toward the doors.

"Probably checking her bag seventeen times to make sure she has everything," Maya said. "You know how she is."

As if on cue, Amber emerged from the doors, pulling a huge suitcase and looking slightly frazzled. Her mousy-brown hair was pulled back in a ponytail, and she wore running shorts and a faded gymnastics t-shirt from some long-ago competition. She'd always been the athlete in our group—the one doing roundoffs in the hallway, the one who could do a standing backflip off the diving board. But something about her seemed different. Thinner, maybe.

"Sorry, sorry!" she called out, rushing toward us. "I thought I lost my phone, but it was in my pocket the whole time."

"Classic Amber," Leah said, pulling her into a hug.

"Don't start with me, Leah. I'm already stressed." She sounded exasperated, but there was a hint of playfulness in her eyes.

Now that we were all together, Maya turned to me, her voice softening. "Lisa, how are you doing? Really?"

The laughter died down. They all looked at me with those careful, concerned faces.

"I'm okay," I said quickly.

"We're so sorry about your mom," Leah added. "I know you two had a complicated relationship, but still—"

"I know, thanks." I felt that familiar tightness in my chest. "But I really don't want to talk about it this weekend. I just ... I need this to be fun. I need to not think about any of that. Okay?"

Rachel squeezed my shoulder. "Then that's what we'll do."

"We're here for you," Maya said. "Whenever you're ready."

"I know you guys are always by my side. But right now, I'm ready for drinks and a beautiful sunset." I forced some sunshine into my voice. "So can we please get out of this airport?"

Amber linked her arm through mine. "Lead the way, boss."

I grabbed Rachel's bag while Maya helped Amber with hers. "Alright, ladies, let's load up! I've got the perfect beach cruiser waiting for us."

When they saw the Jeep with the top off, Maya gasped. "Oh, this is perfect. Lisa, you thought of everything."

"Just wait until you see the house," I said, feeling proud. I'd planned this down to every detail, and seeing their faces light up made every hour of research worth it.

We loaded their bags into the back—Rachel's bright yellow hard-shell roller bag, Maya's teal green soft-sided case, Leah's sleek plum carry-on that probably cost more than my flight, and Amber's oversized charcoal gray bag that looked like she'd packed for a month.

Rachel called shotgun, which was totally her M.O., and the other three squeezed into the back seat. As soon as we were all in, I connected my phone to Bluetooth.

"I made us a playlist," I announced.

"Of course you did," Maya said warmly.

AC/DC's "Back in Black" came on, and, without missing a beat, all five of us started singing along—badly, loudly, joyfully.

This was what I needed. Not thinking about my mother. Not thinking about death or grief or any of it. Just my best friends, terrible singing, and the California sunshine.

As we merged onto the 101 heading toward the beach, I caught Rachel watching me from the passenger seat. She didn't say anything, just gave me a small smile—the kind that said: *I see you. I know you're hurting. But I'm not going to push.*

I smiled back and cranked up the music louder.

The wind whipped through our hair as we drove down the coast. Maya was taking selfies in the back seat. Leah was filming the ocean views for Instagram. Amber had her eyes closed, face tilted toward the sun.

"This is already the best weekend ever!" Maya shouted over the music.

And for the first time since I'd watched my mother take her last breath, I thought maybe—just maybe—I might actually be okay.

When we pulled up to the Airbnb, the girls gasped.

"Lisa, this place is gorgeous!"

"Right on the beach! You outdid yourself!"

"I knew you guys were going to love it!" I was beaming.

They grabbed their bags and headed inside.

I said, "There are three rooms. I haven't put my stuff away yet. You girls pick your rooms, and I'll just take whatever's left."

They all headed downstairs, chattering excitedly. Leah and Maya, who had practically lived together in high school, shared a room. Amber and Rachel took the second room.

"Lisa! These coffee cups are adorable!" Leah said as she led the group back upstairs.

"They look just like us! And the masks," said Rachel, "that's so incredibly thoughtful of you!"

I could tell by the looks on their faces that they felt special. Their joy made the hours of planning so worth it.

"We left you the master bedroom," said Amber.

"You didn't have to do that. I really don't mind sharing with someone."

"No, Lisa, you planned this amazing trip and got us here in one piece. You've paid for almost everything, and now, you're showering us with gifts. You absolutely deserve the biggest bedroom, all to yourself. It's the least we could do to thank you for all you've done."

We unpacked our things, changed into comfortable clothes, and reconvened in the living room. The couch faced the ocean through floor-to-ceiling windows. The sound of waves provided a constant, soothing backdrop.

"Okay, so what's the plan?" Amber asked, curling up on one end of the couch.

I pulled out my phone. "I've got a few ideas. Tomorrow I thought we could check out the Lavender Festival in Ojai— it's supposed to be amazing. But tonight, I was thinking we should just hang out here. I'll cook, and we can catch up. What do you think?"

"Perfect," Maya said.

"I'm starving," Amber added.

"When are you not starving?" Rachel teased.

"Well, chickies, I can fix that problem!" I said as I made a beeline for the kitchen.

I stood at the kitchen island, tossing spiralized zucchini with pesto, feeling like a million bucks. Food was my love language. And cooking here, in this open kitchen full of chatter and music and clinking glasses, was my kind of therapy. The smell of garlic, fresh pesto, and roasted tomatoes filled the air.

Leah and Maya had wandered in to help, though "help" mostly meant picking at the grilled bread and sipping their wine while dancing barefoot to Pat Benatar. Rachel fished out the wedge of Parmesan and started shaving it directly over the zucchini.

Noticing the wine bottle was getting low, I asked, "Maya, will you open another bottle of red? But don't pour any for me. I'm gonna make a batch of my famous Loopie's Lemonade. Any takers?"

"Loopie's Lemonade?" Rachel repeated, eyebrow raised. "Do I want one?"

"You definitely want one."

"What's in it?" Maya asked.

"Tequila, fresh lemonade, and a splash of cranberry."

"Oh, yum, yes, sign me up!" Rachel said. "Just a small one, though. That's about all the hard liquor I can handle these days."

"You know, I haven't made this in forever, but when I was back in college, I used to make it all the time. The regulars always called me by my nickname, so they'd come in and ask for Loopie's Lemonade. The name stuck!"

"Pour one for me, too. I wanna taste it." Leah stopped Amber on her way out of the bathroom. "Amber, what do you want to drink during dinner?"

"Just water for me," Amber walked past us toward the window.

As she stared at the ocean, the rest of us exchanged quick glances. I'd given them all the heads-up that Amber wasn't drinking anymore, but, thankfully, no one made it weird.

I called out above the noise of the kitchen, "I've also got sparkling water, kombucha, or fresh-squeezed lemonade."

"A little lemonade sounds perfect. Thanks, Lisa."

"I've got you, Amb."

By the time the table was set, accented with flowers I'd picked from outside and two candles from the store, we were all famished.

We raised a toast before the first bite.

"To girlfriends who will love each other, no matter what."

The food disappeared fast, accompanied by satisfied sighs and requests for seconds. "Lisa, this pesto is incredible," Maya said, sopping up the last bit with her bread.

Rachel couldn't get over the spiralized zucchini—"It's like healthy pasta!"—and made me promise to show her how to make it.

We lingered long after the sun dipped behind the horizon. Maya put her napkin on the table and relaxed into her chair. "Remember when we all had perms and Sun-In and thought we looked like Madonna?"

Amber chimed in, "Speak for yourself. I looked like a burnt Q-tip."

Laughter exploded around the table, and the stories began spilling out.

"We were so awkward. But I swear, we were fearless," I said, wiping away happy tears. "Let's take this party to the living room. Anyone need a refill?"

Leah got up first. "That sounds like the best idea of the night! This wine is so good! I'm going to have to pace myself, though. Maybe it's from traveling, but I've already got a buzz."

As the rest of us moved from the table, Amber pulled out her phone. "I have to make a quick phone call. I'll be back in a few minutes." She walked out onto the deck and closed the door behind her.

We headed to the giant sectional couch, with the windows wide open to the sea breeze. I pulled out the yearbooks. Their covers were worn at the edges, and they were filled with messages and phone numbers. Every cute guy had been circled.

We passed them around, sharing the memories that were popping up.

Maya flipped to the choir concert photo. "Do you remember when the wrong soundtrack played? It was the rehearsal track, and it already had all the singing on it?"

"And we started singing anyway, so the sound guy turned off our mics!" Amber added. "It turned into a lip-sync concert!"

"I thought Mrs. Henderson was going to have a coronary," Leah said.

"Girl," I said, "I have never lip-synced so convincingly in my life!"

Rachel wiped her eyes. "The parents had no idea. They thought we sounded great."

Maya almost choked on her drink. "My mom told me afterward that I had 'really projected.' Ma'am, I was mouthing the words!"

I was laughing so hard that I had to set my drink down to keep from spilling it.

Amber came back in quietly and found a spot next to Leah.

"Nice of you to join us!" Leah teased.

"Yeah, we all go across the country to come together after years apart, and Amber is hanging out on her phone! We're not seventeen anymore, Amber," Rachel said.

As Amber looked down, I noticed something behind her eyes. A sadness, maybe?

"We're just kidding," said Maya. "Everything ok?"

"Yep. There was just something I had to do. It's all good now."

We dug back into the yearbooks. As the pages turned, we shared story after story that made us laugh so hard we couldn't breathe, doubled over on the couch. Just like in high school, I peed my pants while in hysterics and had to go change.

When I got back, I saw Amber pull a folded slip of notebook paper from between the pages. "Look at this note from Greg!" She cranked up the drama. "Dear Lisa, we belong together. Will you marry me?"

"Uh," I said, "that didn't work out so well. Greg and I were close, but he never struck me as marriage material. Soooo glad I didn't accept his proposal because now he's married ... to a *man*."

Amber's eyes went wide. "Whoa! Dodged that bullet!"

In the background, my playlist rolled on: Heart, Taylor Dane, The Go-Go's. We sang. We danced. We refilled our drinks.

As the night wore on, Leah looked around at all of us, and her eyes got a little shiny. "I can't believe we let this much time go by. Like, why don't we do this more often?"

"Because we're idiots?" Maya offered.

Leah smiled. "I mean it though. We text, but it's not the same. I miss you girls. But you know how it is—we get so absorbed in our children's lives. We get conditioned to convenience, you know? It's way easier to meet someone for a walk down the street or at the park than it is to actually plan a whole weekend away. And I'm sorry for not being better about that with all of you. We've missed so many years together—let's not miss any more."

"We're here now," I said.

"I know. And I don't want to wait for forever to do it again."

"Then we won't," Rachel said simply. "We'll make this a thing. Annual girls' trip."

"Yes!" Maya raised her hand. "I'm already planning next year's playlist."

"You're not in charge of the playlist," I protested.

"I absolutely am. You had your turn."

In a single evening, we had fallen back into our rhythm. Forty-plus years of friendship, and it felt like no time had passed at all.

Later, after everyone had gone to bed, I stood at the kitchen sink rinsing wine and cocktail glasses. I looked at my reflection staring back at me from the window. For just a moment, I let my guard down.

I was so tired. Packing up my mom's life had been grueling. I had to be strong, be the one who had it all together. I was tired of pretending my mother's death hadn't cracked something open inside me.

And angry that even in death, my mom still had some control over how I acted.

But tomorrow we'd go to Ojai. We'd laugh and shop and eat too much. I'd keep it together. I always did.

I dried my hands and headed to bed. As soon as I walked into my quiet room, something on my pillow caught my attention. A small, pink organza gift bag. Beside it, a miniature white envelope so tiny it could've come from a dollhouse. Through the bag, I could see a beaded bracelet with a large silver peace sign in the middle.

As I opened up the drawstring and slipped on the colorful bracelet, I knew who it was from: Leah. It was so perfect and well put together. Her elegant handwriting on the note simply said, "Thanks for all you do! Leah."

Leah is the most private of all of us. I'm the opposite. I made an event out of the gift-giving and waited for the sound of excitement, but she did this quietly. Only I would know about her thoughtfulness. It's just her way. Has been since we were twelve. Some things never change.

As I turned around to put the bracelet on the nightstand, I caught sight of my suitcase sitting in the corner, still partially packed from Sacramento. I should unpack it properly and hang things up. But I couldn't bring myself to open it all the way. Not yet.

Some baggage, I'd learned, was easier to leave half-packed.

Two

The next morning, we woke to the golden California sunshine streaming through patchy fog as it made its way to the windows. Over coffee on the deck, I reminded everyone about our plan.

"Ojai today, right?" Rachel asked, stretching.

"Yep. The Lavender Festival. I've been wanting to go to Ojai for years, and this is the perfect excuse to go."

"I'm in," Maya said. "As long as there's food."

"When is there not food?" Leah teased.

We packed up the Jeep with essentials—water, snacks, and sweatshirts in case the temperature dropped. By 9 a.m., we were on the road. The fog had completely dissipated.

We took the 101 and then turned onto Highway 150. The road twisted through the beautiful rolling hills, giving us a view that was more desolate but still stunning.

I cranked up the "Santa Barbara Babes" playlist. Air Supply's "All Out of Love" blasted through the speakers.

"Oh God, this song," Leah groaned from the back seat.

"What's wrong with this song?" I asked, defensive.

"Nothing's wrong with it. I just have trauma from eighth grade when Tommy Martinez dedicated it to me at Sunrise Roller Rink and then went right over to Jennifer Parker and asked her to couples skate."

We all burst out laughing.

"Tommy Martinez was an idiot," Maya said. "Remember when he tried to bleach his hair and it turned orange?"

"He looked like a traffic cone," said Amber.

Rachel turned around to face them. "He peaked in eighth grade."

The wind whipped through our hair as we climbed higher into the hills.

"Want to stop at the next lookout point?"

Unanimous agreement. We couldn't resist.

I pulled over. "Let's do a group photo here. It's gorgeous!"

We hopped out, and the wind immediately attacked us, blowing our hair into our faces.

Leah looked at Amber and lost it. "Amber, your hair looks like one of those troll hair pencil toppers we had in middle school! I didn't know hair could stick straight up like that in real life!"

"Help me fix it, you guys!"

Leah and Maya patted down Amber's hair as we came together for the picture.

"Oh shoot! My hair is stuck to my lip gloss," I said, twisting my blonde mop into a messy bun.

We snapped a few pictures, windblown hair and all, capturing the moment and the start of what we thought would be a gorgeous Saturday.

The quaint town of Ojai welcomed us with perfect walking weather. With temperatures hovering around seventy-five degrees, I was glad we'd arrived early. The Lavender Festival was already packed with people—it felt like a Fourth of July parade, but with lavender everywhere. Lavender clothes, lavender hair accessories, lavender jewelry, even lavender ice cream.

I was in heaven. Every cute boutique we passed, I wanted to go in and try things on. The girls were good sports about it, following me from store to store.

I wrapped a lavender-and-cream infinity scarf around my neck. "Whoa! This is so soft! Rachel, how does it look?"

She shrugged. "Like another scarf you don't need."

"You're right, you're right." I took off the scarf and kept looking for the perfect souvenir.

At the third boutique, I found it—matching lavender t-shirts with "Lavender Ladies" written in swirly purple script across the front, with tiny lavender sprigs scattered around the letters.

"We sooooo have to get these!" I squealed, holding one up.

Maya took one look and started laughing. "Are you serious right now?"

"Come on! It'll be so fun!"

"Lisa, that is the tackiest thing I've ever seen," Leah said, wrinkling her nose. "I wouldn't be caught dead in that."

"It's not tacky, it's cute! It's kitschy!"

"It's the same thing," Leah said firmly.

"I'll wear one," Amber offered, ever the peacemaker.

"Thank you, Amber!" I said triumphantly.

"I'll wear one too," Maya said. "What the hell. We're on vacation."

Rachel caved. "Fine. But I'm not wearing it in public after today."

We all looked at Leah.

"Absolutely not," she said. "I have a professional reputation to maintain."

"We're in Ojai! Who's going to see you?" I protested.

"I post everything on Instagram. My clients follow me. I'm not posting myself in a t-shirt that says 'Lavender Ladies' like I'm in a geriatric bowling league."

Knowing she wouldn't budge, I said, "Fine. But you're missing out."

We bought four shirts and put them on in the changing room. Leah, true to form, bought an elegant lavender silk scarf.

By lunchtime, we were starving, so we found a cute Italian restaurant tucked down a side street. As we walked through the door, Maya stopped short.

"Kim?"

"Maya?" said Kim. "Oh, my goodness! Amber, Rachel, Leah, and wow, Lisa! What are you guys doing here? Nice shirts!"

Leah rolled her eyes. "Please don't get them started on the shirt thing!"

I recognized her immediately—Kim Jennings. She'd been on the drill team with some of us back in high school. Time had changed her—it changed all of us, but she just looked … different. Her smile was still the same though.

She wore faded jeans with an intentionally frayed hem and a lavender beaded top that looked artisanal, like something she might have just picked up at one of the shops across the street. Her jewelry was stunning—big, chunky silver pieces that looked worn but could have just as easily been brand new. I noticed that among all of her rings, a wedding ring wasn't one of them.

"Great to see you, Kim! Do you live here?" I asked.

"No, I still live in Sac. I treated myself to a trip down here because I'm celebrating my divorce—finally!" She gave us a practiced victory pose.

"Oh shoot, I'm sorry ... or not sorry?" Maya asked, unsure. Her hand stilled on the strap of her purse. I caught the slight tension in her shoulders, the way her expression changed for just a moment—something I recognized but couldn't quite name.

"Yeah, definitely not sorry. It's a good thing." Kim let out a nervous laugh. "Actually, it's a great thing."

"Maya, let Kim answer that over lunch. I can change our number from five to six," I said. "Kim, will you join us?"

"Oh, wow! That's so nice of you all! Yeah, I would love to join you, thanks!"

The hostess walked us to a nice, big, round table tucked in a quiet corner of the restaurant. We settled in as she handed out menus. Even though the restaurant was full, the high ceilings allowed us to hear each other over the hum of conversation and clinking dishes.

I glanced at the menu briefly—everything looked good—but I was more interested in catching up with Kim than deciding between pasta options.

The server came to take our drink orders. "We have a special lavender cosmopolitan if you'd like to try it," she suggested.

"Ooh, that sounds amazing!" I said. "I'll have one of those."

Rachel, Maya, and Leah all ordered the same.

Amber folded her hands around her water glass. "I'll have a sparkling water with lime, please."

As our waitress walked away, Kim said, "Before I tell you what's been going on with me, I want to hear about all of *you!* I know it's hard to sum up the last thirty years, but tell me about your lives now."

Rachel broke the ice. "Well, I just retired. I was a middle school principal for twenty years, but I had to stop because of breast cancer treatment. I'm in remission now, thank God, but with surgery and chemo and radiation ... it was time."

"Oh, Rachel, I'm so sorry you went through that," Kim said, reaching across the table to squeeze her hand. "But I'm glad you're okay now."

"Me too."

Pulling her hand back, Kim asked, "Are you glad to be retired?"

"Ask me again in a few months," Rachel said with a small laugh. "I'm still figuring out what to do with myself."

Kim was full of questions. "Do you have kids?"

"Two daughters. And an amazing husband," Rachel answered.

Maya jumped in. "I've got two teenagers at home—well, when they're not with their dad. I got divorced about six months ago."

"Oof. So sorry," said Kim, shaking her head.

Maya shrugged, but her expression changed. "It's fine. Better this way."

"Are you still a nurse?"

"Yep. Working at St. Mary's in the ER. It's crazy, but I love it."

"And I'm doing interior design," Leah added. "Residential, mostly. High-end homes. Business is good, but it keeps me running. My daughter Hannah is a fitness influencer—very successful, which is wonderful, but also ..." she trailed off. "It's complicated."

"Is anything really ever simple?" Kim asked. "I think everyone's story is complicated. What about you, Amber? Didn't you go to college for gymnastics?"

We all looked at Amber, who got a wistful look on her face. "I did," she said. "I had a full-ride scholarship to the University of Oklahoma—"

"I remember you being really, really good," Kim interrupted.

Amber blushed. "It was my dream to compete and, eventually, to coach. But my body had other plans. I fell off the uneven bars and broke my back in a competition. That pretty much ended my sports career.

"I have a daughter who competes, so at least I still get a dose of the gymnastics world. I decided to become a hairstylist to pay the bills, but ..." she seemed to hesitate, "right now, I'm working part-time at a community center. I, um ... I left the salon."

"How long were you doing hair?" Kim asked.

"Almost twenty-five years," Amber said. "It was time for a change."

Something about the way she said it felt careful, as if she was choosing her words. Rachel glanced at me, and I caught the question in her eyes: *Do you know what's going on with her?* I shook my head slightly.

"Well, sometimes a change is good," Kim said warmly. "New chapters and all that."

"Yeah," Amber said quietly. "Something like that."

Deciding to break the tension, I piped up. "As for me, I have a full plate! I'm a serial entrepreneur. I never stop moving and creating. I have two kids, and my husband, who used to play in the NFL, sometimes makes three in total."

Rachel gave me a knowing wink.

Kim put her napkin in her lap and started placing her silverware. "You all seem like you're doing well. I mean, life is messy for everyone, right? But you have each other. That's the important thing."

The way she said it gave me a tight feeling in my chest. She seemed to be genuinely happy for us, even though she had just gone through a divorce. That had to be so hard.

Eager to catch up with Kim, I said, "Okay, that's us in a nutshell. Kim, what about you? You seem really happy."

"Aw, thanks. I've actually been on quite the roller coaster ride since high school. It's a long story—I'm not sure how much you want to hear."

Leah, who hadn't said much since we sat down, leaned forward. "We all have baggage, girl. Let 'er rip, we've got all day."

Kim let out a short laugh. "You're right. We all have our thing, don't we? Let's see … remember Paul? We were still dating when we graduated high school. Great guy. Probably should've stayed with him.

"About four years after we broke up, I worked as a cocktail waitress for a little while, and that's when I met this guy named William. 'Wicked Willie' is what I ended up calling him in my mind. He eventually wrecked everything in my life."

That got our attention.

"At first, we were so in love. He was in the construction business, and things were good. But a few years after we got married, he had to have surgery on his left shoulder. All those years of carrying lumber from the truck to the site caused a lot of wear and tear and damage to his nerves and muscles. After the surgery, he healed, but the pain never went away, so he drank to cope. Jack Daniel's became his friend, but it definitely wasn't mine."

Amber's fingers tightened around her water glass. I caught a glimpse of her expression changing from concern to something else. A flicker of recognition, maybe? Or memory?

"After about eight years of marriage, he started to get controlling—really bad. At first, I didn't think much of it because my dad was also pretty controlling." Kim's voice grew softer as she continued.

"Then he became abusive. Mentally, physically, sexually. The works. It's the most horrible thing I've ever experienced in my life. I didn't know how to get out."

All five of us sat there, jaws dropped in shock. Maya spoke for all of us: "Oh wow, Kim, we're so sorry."

"Thanks. It really started one night when he came home drunk and expected dinner, but it was so late that I'd already put it away."

Kim's expression darkened as she recounted the memory. "He came through the front door, shouting, 'Kim! I'm starving. Where's my damn dinner? Did you even fucking make anything for me, you piece of shit?'

"I couldn't believe he was talking to me like that. It was so awful."

"Do you know what changed?" Rachel asked. "What made him act so mean and vulgar?"

"To this day, I still don't know. I think it might have been a mix of the meds after surgery, the alcohol, the decline of his business, and the constant pain … I really don't know. But that night was the beginning of the worst."

"Oh, Kim, what did you—" Amber asked, her voice faint.

"I was terrified, shaking. I had made dinner and put a covered plate for him in the fridge because I thought it was too late for him to eat and assumed he'd have grabbed something while he was out with his buddies. I just pulled out the plate and heated it up in the microwave. I didn't say a word—I was too scared. After he ate, he passed out in our bed, and I ended up sleeping on the couch—or rather, I parked myself on the couch. I don't know how much sleep I actually got that night.

"For the next seventeen years, it was a constant cycle of him hitting me, yelling at me, calling me names. He rarely had a kind word. When he was sober, he'd sometimes apologize, saying he wouldn't do it again, but it never stopped."

I saw Leah close her eyes for just a second. When she opened them, they were glassy.

"I felt so trapped, like I was living in a straitjacket."

"Here you go, ladies. Lavender cosmos …" Our waitress arrived and the spell lifted. Sound flooded back in. We exhaled all at once, as if we'd forgotten to breathe.

"Are you ready to order, or should I come back in a few?"

"We haven't looked at the menus yet," I managed. "Can you give us a few more minutes?"

"Of course, take your time." The waitress glanced at the serious faces around the table and quietly backed away.

No one reached for their drink. We were all still processing what Kim had just told us.

Kim seemed completely unaware of the waitress or the people around us. "I tried to leave for years. And all that time, I was scared to death of getting pregnant. Can you even imagine?"

Maya asked, "How did you finally get away from him? I mean … if you don't mind me asking."

I knew Maya had recently gotten divorced, but I didn't know the details. Maya's voice was steady, but something told me she genuinely understood what it took to finally leave.

"I don't mind. Honestly, I've been carrying this around for so long. It feels like ... relief, almost. To just say it."

Kim took a moment to gather her thoughts.

"He hit me so hard one night with the back of his hand. When his knuckles smacked against my face, I thought I was going to pass out."

She pointed to her right eye, making a circling motion. "He broke my orbital bone—you know, the eye socket. It was the most excruciating pain—I'd never felt anything like it. I wouldn't wish that on my worst enemy."

Listening to Kim felt like reading a novel, but it was her real life.

"When he saw my eye, all the blood, and heard my screams, I think it sobered him up for a moment—to the point where he actually drove me to the ER and just dropped me off."

We sat in stunned silence, hanging on her every word. It suddenly made sense why she looked different to me. Her right eye drooped a bit in the corner.

"The nurses were in a panic because of the amount of blood on my face. The cops came in a while later to interview me—because who shows up with a broken eye socket without abuse being involved? I spent almost a week in the hospital, recovering, and Wicked Willie spent a month in jail until his sister finally bailed him out."

"Dear God," Amber said under her breath.

"When he was in jail, his sister and I talked about what the future would look like. We agreed that he would go to rehab and anger-management counseling, and I went straight to our attorney to file for divorce. I hired someone to serve him the papers, and he signed them on the spot. I haven't spoken to him since, and I don't plan to."

"I second that," I said. The five of us looked like we just walked out of a horror movie–stunned, sad, and relieved she got out.

"Thank you. It's over now, and I'm just so happy to be here. That's why I'm here in Ojai—it's a place I've always wanted to visit. The spas, Sundance, this Lavender Festival—William would never let me come here."

She looked around the table at each of us, then down at her drink, stirring it slowly. "I thought this would be the perfect escape and a celebration of finally being free from Wicked Willie."

We grabbed our drinks and raised them high.

"Cheers to you, Kim, to the end of an era of pain, and to the beginning of the rest of your life," I said.

We clinked glasses, the sound crisp and final, like punctuation at the end of a sentence.

The conversation shifted after that, deliberately lighter. We ordered lunch—pasta and salads and way too much bread.

When the check came, I insisted on paying. "Today's on me, Kim. All of it."

"You don't have to do that, Lisa."

"I know. But I want to."

Outside the restaurant, we lingered for a moment in the afternoon sunshine. Kim pulled each of us into a hug, holding on just a beat longer than casual friends would.

"Thank you for this," she said. "For listening and not making me feel crazy."

"You're not crazy," Maya said firmly. "You're brave."

Kim's eyes filled, and she blinked the tears away quickly. "You guys are the first people I've told the whole story to—well, besides my therapist. It helps that you knew me before all of that mess. I didn't realize how much I needed that."

After we exchanged numbers and promised to stay in touch—promises I think we all actually meant this time—Kim headed toward the spa she'd booked for herself. We watched her walk away. Her shoulders were a little straighter than when we'd first seen her.

"That could have been any of us," Leah said quietly.

She was right, and it was sobering.

We spent the rest of the afternoon at the festival, but things felt different. We still laughed about the vendors selling lavender-flavored everything, and we still took silly photos with our arms around each other. But there were moments of unexpected quiet, too. Times when one of us would get lost in thought while the others pretended not to notice.

The live music was beautiful. A woman with a guitar sang about seasons changing and second chances, and I caught Amber wiping her eyes during the song. Maya stood with her arms crossed, staring at something in the distance that probably wasn't there.

I wanted to ask them what they were thinking. But I didn't. Whatever Kim's story had stirred up, they'd share when they were ready.

The drive back to the house was quiet. That morning, we'd been singing, laughing, and pointing out landmarks. Now, nobody even reached for the radio. I checked the rearview mirror—Maya was staring out at the hills, but I don't think she was seeing them. Rachel had her eyes closed in the passenger seat, though I could tell she wasn't asleep.

By the time we pulled up to the beach house, the sun was starting its slow descent toward the water, painting everything gold. We grabbed our bags and festival purchases—the lavender soap and candles we'd convinced ourselves we needed—and headed inside.

I set my bags on the counter and opened my mouth to suggest dinner, but the words didn't come. The kitchen suddenly felt too small, too enclosed. After Kim's story, after that heavy drive home, the thought of being inside cooking a huge meal felt wrong.

Amber must have felt it too, because she spoke up first. "Does anyone else feel like just ... being outside?"

Maya immediately stood up. "I bet the sunset is going to be gorgeous. Let's watch it."

"Beach fire and snacks?" Rachel suggested.

I chimed in. "I'll grab the charcuterie stuff!"

We moved through the kitchen with quiet efficiency. I put together the board: sliced salami, prosciutto, and four different cheeses—chunks, triangles, slices. A small bowl of pesto, a bit of honey, and truffle mustard. Three types of crackers surrounded by candied pecans, provincial almonds, and seedless grapes. A few sprigs of rosemary to finish it off.

Maya grabbed glasses while Leah collected blankets from the living room. Amber filled a small cooler with drinks and ice.

Outside, the beach was nearly empty. The tourists had cleared out for dinner, leaving us with the sounds of waves and seagulls. Rachel and Leah grabbed the portable firepit under the house and moved it onto the sand.

"Okay, so who actually knows how to build a fire?" Rachel asked, hands on her hips, staring at the fire pit.

"I know this will come as a shock," I said, "but I can build a fire in a snowstorm! I'll have one going in no time!"

"Geez," Leah said, "trip planner, gourmet cook, and now fire expert. What can't you do?"

"I've just learned to do a lot of different stuff," I said, arranging the wood.

"She alphabetizes her spice cabinet," Rachel teased.

"Wait, alphabetically? Really?" Amber looked at me.

"And her closet is organized by season and color," Rachel added.

"Okay, I get it, I'm—"

"Type A?" Maya finished. "Yeah, we noticed."

I tossed a stick in her direction. "Can we please focus on the actual fire?"

"Oh, we're focused," Maya said, dodging it. "The Lisa Najarian Show is very entertaining."

Within minutes, I had a perfect fire going. The girls applauded mockingly, and it felt good to laugh after the heaviness of the day.

We spread out the blankets and settled in around the flames. We picked at the cheese, sipped our drinks, and watched the fire.

The sun sank lower, turning the sky pink and orange.

Nobody spoke for a long time, until Rachel finally broke the silence. "I can't stop thinking about Kim."

"Me neither," Leah said.

"Any one of us could have met the wrong person at the right time," Rachel continued. "Or stayed in a bad situation because we couldn't figure out how to leave …"

Amber was staring into the fire, her face unreadable.

"It makes you think about what we all carry around, doesn't it?" I said carefully. "The things we don't talk about."

Maya pulled a blanket into her lap. "Yeah. It does."

"Maya?" Leah said tenderly. "You okay?"

Maya laughed, but it came out shaky. "I don't know. I keep thinking about what Kim said. About feeling trapped. About choosing never to have kids because of her situation." She hesitated. "I chose to have kids. I wanted them so badly. But my marriage ..."

She looked around at all of us—her oldest friends, the women who'd known her since she was twelve years old. Shadows from the fire danced across her face.

"I got divorced six months ago," she said quietly. "And people keep asking me—are you okay? Are you sad? Are you angry? And I just ... I don't even know. Some days I'm crying. Some days, I'm so scared I can barely function. And then, other days, I wake up excited about something, and then I feel like shit for being excited. Who does that? Who gets excited that their marriage is over?" She looked up at us. "But I do. And I have no idea who I'm even supposed to be anymore."

We all went very still.

Rachel shifted closer to Maya and put her arm around her shoulders. "You're Maya. That's who you are."

"But what does that even mean anymore?" Maya whispered.

The fire crackled. The ocean crashed. And we all leaned in, ready to listen.

Three

"What do you mean, you don't know who you are?" Rachel asked with a look of concern.

The fire popped, sending a small shower of sparks into the dark sky. I pulled my sweatshirt up around my neck.

Maya shook her head. "When we separated, I thought that life would go on just as it always had, just without Mark in the mix. But that's not what happened. Everything is different. I think differently. I live differently. The way I make decisions is different. It's not us anymore—it's just me. And I've realized that somewhere in the last twenty years, I kind of lost who I am."

"It's got to be disorienting," said Amber.

"You have no idea, Amber. This is unknown territory for me. I've been a wife … a mom … a nurse … I'm really good at being whatever I need to be for the people around me. But who do I want to be? Because I'm not the old me anymore."

Rachel shifted on the blanket. "Can we ask what happened? With the divorce?"

Maya thought for a minute. "Where do I even start?" The ocean crashed steadily behind us. "Mark and I worked hard to build the life we thought we were supposed to have. The house, the careers, the kids. We were both running hard—I stepped in as charge nurse at the hospital, and Mark was pulling long hours at his consulting firm. But it was paying off. Things were good. We even had the white picket fence."

"I always thought you had the perfect family," Amber said. "You and Mark, both so successful, that gorgeous house, two beautiful kids. I kind of envied you. Everything just seemed to work so well for you guys."

Maya shrugged. "It looked great, didn't it? But we were so busy working that family life became something we had to fit in. We both worked long hours, and our schedules never lined up. You know how shift work is. But we were making it work—or at least, I thought we were."

Maya watched a couple walk by them along the beach, thoughtful.

"First, he started spending money. Tailored suits. A Porsche. More expensive watches. He started spending more and more time at the office. He said they'd picked up this huge new client, and the workload was insane."

She looked up at us.

"Turns out the 'client' was a twenty-two-year-old intern at his firm. Fresh out of college, hoping to work her way into a full-time position."

"Sounds like she got her full-time position," Rachel said dryly.

"Geez, Mark. Tell me you're having a midlife crisis *without* telling me you're having a midlife crisis," Leah muttered.

"*Twenty-two*, you guys," Maya's voice cracked. "She could be our daughter."

"That's so gross," Amber said.

"At first, when I found out, I felt like a failure. Like I wasn't good enough to keep him happy. Wasn't young enough, fun enough, exciting enough. He'd traded me in for a newer model."

Maya stared into the flames, her face illuminated by the orange glow. "But then I met her. At Zoe's graduation. He brought her. Can you believe it?"

"He didn't!" I smacked my leg.

"Yep. Dad of the year. And, of course, I couldn't look away. She was wearing a sundress that was waaaay too short, giggling at his jokes, hanging on his arm—and I stopped feeling bad. I started feeling pissed. The whole thing was ridiculous. He humiliated me. He tore up our family. And for what? That silly little girl?"

"I remember how crazy we were at that age," I said. "That was fun and all, but you couldn't pay me to go back to being twenty-two. She might look cute in that sundress, but can you imagine the conversations? What do they even talk about? His colonoscopy and her TikTok followers?"

Maya deadpanned, "I wonder if she's discovered yet that he sleeps with a CPAP machine."

"Oh my—" Leah gasped between giggles.

"Can you imagine?" I wheezed. "Nothing says sexy like Darth Vader breathing."

Rachel wiped her eyes. "Yeah, twenty-two. He was thinking with something other than his head on that one. Maybe he thinks she'll be easier to control. But boy, is he in for a surprise. He has no idea how much control he gave up."

"What blows me away," said Maya, "is the selfishness of it all. It astounds me. I don't think it has even occurred to him what this is doing to his daughters. How they feel."

"How are they?" Rachel asked.

"Confused. And disgusted. Zoe said, 'Mom, she's the same age as some of the girls in the sorority that I want to be in.' She doesn't want to be seen with them. But he doesn't care. All he cares about is his new arm-candy."

"I'm so sorry they're going through that," Rachel said.

"So, the divorce was the easy part. I didn't think twice. This wasn't the man I had married. Mark used to be ...

he was a good guy. We had a partnership. But somewhere along the way, he became this cliché—the middle-aged man chasing youth, buying a sports car, dating someone half his age. I no longer recognized him. And I couldn't respect or love this version of him. I didn't want to do life with him anymore."

"Are you still angry?" Amber asked.

"It depends on which minute you ask me. Sometimes, yes, I'm furious. I can't believe he just threw away twenty-five years of marriage without at least *trying* to fix it. I was really busy with work and the kids, and we were kind of on autopilot, but I had no idea our marriage was that far gone. We could have gone to counseling.

"Sometimes I still feel embarrassed. I feel so stupid that this huge change happened right under my nose. And then I get sad. He blew up our family, and the kids are hurting. That tears me up inside. How could he do that to us?

"Then the next minute, I'm actually relieved. I can't stand the person he's become, and I'm glad I don't have to put up with his crap anymore. And then I feel guilty for being glad. Like, my marriage ended. Shouldn't I be more broken up about it?"

"You can be all those things at the same time," Rachel offered. "They're not mutually exclusive. But it's got to be hard to let go of the man you thought he was and accept who he is—or at least who he appears to be."

"Yeah, all of those feelings are just ... swirling around," Maya said. "And here's the thing: I spend my waking hours helping people, fixing problems, making everything better. But I can't fix myself. I feel everything all at once, and I don't know what to do with any of it."

The fire had burned down some, and the wind was picking up. I noticed Maya shivering slightly, hugging herself.

"But the thing that surprised me most is that it woke me up. I can't believe how numb I'd gotten. Honestly, I haven't felt much of anything these last couple of years. Take care of the house, go to the girls' events at school, go to work and spend twelve hours just trying to get a five-minute break to pee, get home starving because I didn't have time to eat at work, throw together some food to keep everyone fed, then practically pass out at bedtime. I really was on autopilot."

The ocean crashed behind us, steady and relentless.

"All of this hurt like hell, but it kind of felt good to finally feel something again, ya know?"

"Hey, passion is passion," I said. "Even if what you're passionate about is kicking him in the balls."

Maya snorted. "Lisa!"

"You could passionately key his new Porsche," said Leah.

"I've definitely thought about it," Maya said, laughing through her tears. "But all those bad feelings are exhausting.

I need a change in my life, and I need to feel good again. And it's scary because I have no idea where to even begin."

"So, what kind of change are you talking about?" Leah asked. "Like, a different career?"

"I've thought about it. I got a pretty good chunk of money from the divorce. Maybe I need to make a radical change, ya know? But is that even a good thought, or am I just going through my own midlife crisis?"

"Why do you say that?" Rachel asked.

"We always tell our patients never to make major decisions right after a bad diagnosis—you know, when emotions are running high. But it's been six months, and I still feel like I need to reinvent myself. I just don't want to do something stupid and throw away a perfectly good career that pays the bills.

"And what would I even do? The truth is, I don't even know who I am without him. We were together for thirty years. I went straight from college to marriage to motherhood. I've never just been ... me. I feel like I've lost myself over all these years because my focus has been on everyone else. I've poured my all into everyone but me. But the girls will be gone soon, and now Mark is gone, so what do I do with myself?"

"I totally see that," Amber said. "You know, even when we were growing up, you were always the one taking care of us. Helping us through breakups, listening to us complain about our parents, staying up all night when we were upset. You've always been an amazing caregiver. I think it's time you finally take care of yourself. It's time to figure out who Maya really is."

Maya thought for a moment. "It's an empty feeling. It's kinda like how I felt after college graduation—no more schoolwork to do or classes to attend, so what do I do now? Back then, I figured it out and had a nursing dream. But now it's different. I'm older, and I feel lost without a plan."

"You could do anything," I said. "Move anywhere. Start over completely ..."

"And that's terrifying," Maya said.

"But maybe it's not. Maybe it's actually just exciting," Rachel said. "When you think about it, those two emotions are almost identical—it's just the story you tell yourself about it. So, what if you're really just excited?"

Maya stared at the fire as she considered that for a minute.

"I'd be lying if I said that I haven't felt some excitement at the thought of it," she said, biting her lip. "But I just keep shutting that down because I don't want to be the psychopath who is actually happy about losing her marriage, quitting her job, and starting all over. People are going to think I'm a total nut job. Besides, what would I do?"

"I bet you can figure that out," I said, smiling. "Okay, forget what everyone else thinks. Forget Mark, forget all of it. Let's start somewhere ... Money is no object, fear doesn't exist. If you could do *anything*—what would make *you* happy?"

Maya hesitated, then let out a nervous laugh. "This is going to sound so stupid ..."

"There are no wrong answers. Let us have it."

"I got into baking, and it turned into my biggest hobby. I love it! I'm good at it, and when I'm baking, I go into this zen-like state. It's the only time I feel fully present. And I love how it makes people feel when I bake something special for them."

"She's not kidding," I said. "When Mom passed away last week, Maya shipped me this huge care package—chocolate chip cookies, lemon bars, banana bread, and these incredible cinnamon rolls. My brother and Mom's boyfriend devoured most of it as we worked at getting rid of Mom's crap. It was so good! They wanted to know where it came from so they could order more."

"What kinds of things do you bake, Maya?" Leah asked.

"You know that show, *The Great British Bake Off*? I would totally be on that if I could. I've tried all of it—breads, cakes, biscuits, pastries. I love the challenge of baking. I always make too much, so I put it in the freezer and ship it when someone needs a little extra care." She winked at me.

"Okay," Rachel said, "so far, not sounding stupid at all. Tell us more. How will this look in your new life?"

The fire crackled between us. "I've kind of thought that if I couldn't be a nurse, it would be really cool to have my own bakery."

Maya glanced at each of her friends, expecting to see some smirks. But nobody was laughing.

"So do it," Amber said.

Maya held Amber's gaze. "I can't just ... I mean, I'm a nurse. I don't know anything about running a business. And could the two jobs be more opposite? That's a huge risk to take over something I know nothing about. How would I make it work?"

"But Maya, is it really that different?" I said. "Think about it. You *do* have business skills. You manage the schedule and are in charge of the other nurses—that's management. And the bedside manner you have to have when you're dealing with patients, families, and even the doctors—that's all customer service."

"And if you're smart enough to get a nursing degree, you're smart enough to learn the rest," Amber said. "If anyone can figure it out, it's you."

Maya thought about it. "Are you guys serious? Do you really think I should consider this? I mean, it's only ever been a passing thought."

"Of course you should," Leah said. "And I'll help you design it! What does your bakery look like? What kind of vibe do you want it to have?"

Maya's whole face changed. She sat up straighter. "Okay, so … I need that cozy feel, almost like being wrapped in a blanket in front of a fireplace with a cup of coffee. Like how you feel when you smell freshly baked bread … you know that scent? Not cold and contemporary, but more homey, like a warm hug.

"Exposed brick for sure, to give it that old-world French vibe. Maybe some reclaimed wood from an old barn. Some small round tables and a few long, farm-style ones where people can sit with their laptops and lattes. Oooh, that's a cute name! 'Laptops and Lattes,' but too techy. A few cushy couches that line the windows and a long counter with backless stools where people can watch me work."

"Okay, so, you've clearly had a minute to think about this!" Leah was getting excited now. "Keep going."

Maya started talking faster. "A good espresso machine—not those pod things, a real one. Teas. Fresh flowers on the tables. And a big display case where you can see everything. The croissants, the cakes, the cookies. I want it to smell like dark chocolate and warm butter and fresh coffee the second you walk in."

"That sounds amazing," Amber said, almost drooling.

"It does, doesn't it?" Maya looked almost surprised at herself.

"I can see it already," Leah said, her designer brain clearly already working. "I'm totally going to help you design it."

"It sounds wonderful. And expensive. How much money would I have to sink into it? I don't want to risk losing everything."

"You could start small," Rachel said. "You could keep your nursing job during the week and then get a booth at the Farmer's Market, or maybe team up with a couple of restaurants. Something to get your name out there."

"Or, you could start online. I started small, too," Leah said. "I built my entire business by word of mouth and social media. You could take online orders and build a following."

"It's a little easier to wrap my head around the idea of this if I don't have to quit my job right away," Maya said. "Maybe it would work. But I've spent my life taking care of people. The thought is exciting, but it's still a pretty big stretch for me."

Amber said, "Maya, feeding people with food you made with love—that's still taking care of people. You're not abandoning who you are, you're just doing it differently. You're just moving to a more complete version of yourself."

Maya's smile faltered and then faded. "But what if Mark was right?"

We all looked at her.

"What?" I said.

"What if ... what if I'm not enough? What if I put everything into this and fail, and that proves that I was the problem all along? That I wasn't interesting enough, ambitious enough, young enough—"

And there it was. The real baggage. Not the divorce, not the identity crisis. It was the fear that she wasn't worth betting on.

"Maya, Mark's midlife crisis isn't about you," I said. "Dating a twenty-something isn't about you. That's about *him* and whatever he's running from. You, my friend, are more than enough."

"Agreed," Rachel said. "Mark walked away from something real for something shiny and new. That's his loss. And now you're free to build a whole new life that you want. Not for him, not for your kids—for *you*."

"Yeah, but failure sure would suck right now," Maya said. "What if—"

"What if you succeed?" Amber interrupted. We all looked at her. "Why are you so sure you'll fail?"

Maya opened her mouth, then closed it. "I ... I don't know."

I moved closer to Maya and took both her hands in mine. "Listen to me. You are absolutely enough. And you are worth every risk, every investment, and every big leap. And you know what? Even if you fail—which you won't because you're Maya—but even if you do, we'll be right there for you."

"Nursing jobs aren't going anywhere," Rachel said. "You'll always have that to fall back on if you need it. But Maya …" She paused, her voice catching. "Life's too short. Trust me on that. Don't live with regrets."

We all got very still and stared at the flickering orange glow of the embers in the dying fire.

A single tear ran down Maya's cheek. "You're right, Rachel. You looked death in the face, and I have watched countless patients do the same. There's no time to live small or play it safe." She sat up straight and patted her legs. "I'm going to do it. I'm going to open up my own bakery."

Everyone cheered.

"I'm still terrified."

"Don't worry! We're going to help you," I said. "I'll help you create your brand."

"We're gonna get you up and running on social media so you can start getting followers," Leah said, grinning. "And when you're ready for a location, I'm going to help you design the coolest place in the city to hang out. I'll make sure it's perfect. Watch out, Starbucks!"

"And Amber and I will be your first customers and your biggest fans," Rachel said.

Maya's shoulders dropped as she leaned back. "You guys, thank you. This is the first time since this whole mess started that I'm really looking forward to the future, and I don't even feel guilty about it! You don't know how much I needed this. Heck, I didn't know how much I needed this."

"Good," Rachel said. "You shouldn't feel even a moment of guilt."

A gust of wind made me shiver. The fire had died down to just embers, and the temperature had dropped. I rubbed my arms.

"It's getting really cold out here," I said. "Should we head inside, chickies?"

"Yeah, I'm freezing," Leah agreed, standing and brushing sand off her jeans.

"One more toast first," I said, raising my nearly empty glass. "To Maya. To new beginnings. To taking up space and betting on yourself."

"To Maya," everyone echoed, clinking glasses one more time.

"This is so crazy." Maya put down her drink. "I'm going to open a bakery. I'm actually going to do it."

We gathered up the remnants of the charcuterie board, the empty wine bottles, and the blankets. I kicked sand over the last of the embers, making sure they were fully out. As we walked toward the house, arms full, I noticed Amber had stopped at the edge of the firepit, staring out at the dark ocean.

I walked back to her. "You coming?"

She turned to look at me, and in the dim light I could see tears on her cheeks.

"Yeah. Sorry. I was just thinking."

"About what?"

Amber was quiet for a moment. "About new starts. About how they're hard, but not impossible." She wiped her face. "I guess I just needed that reminder."

I wanted to ask more, but Maya called from the deck, "Come on, you two! I'm freezing, and I hear wine calling my name!"

Amber managed a small laugh and started walking. I fell into step beside her, wondering what she was really thinking about, what she was carrying that we still didn't know about yet.

Four

As we walked in and shut the door, Maya collapsed on the couch and let out a happy sigh. "Ahhh, I love that warm, tingly feeling you get when you come inside from the chilly outdoors."

"Hate to break it to you," Leah said dryly, "but having a warm, tingly feeling usually requires more than a change in temperature."

Maya groaned. "Well, since I'm divorced now, I'll take what I can get."

"Let's get the fire going in the fireplace," Amber said. "Good news, Lisa! The fireplace is gas, so we don't need your superhero fire-starting skills. I can just push the button!"

The other girls laughed as they set down the empty plates, glasses, and bottles and settled in.

"Well, that's a good thing," I answered, "because instead of building a fire, I was thinking of heading into the kitchen and fixing us a light dinner. We still have some of that yummy cheese, and there's bread and salad left over from last night. How about salad and grilled cheese sandwiches? I'll use up my jar of pesto instead of butter."

"More food?" Leah asked. "Do you all normally eat this much?"

"I do, and that sounds amazing," Rachel said. "I'm in!"

"C'mon Leah, your girlish figure won't suffer from a little extra food. Live a little!" I said.

I pulled out the pans and ingredients, and my heart felt full as I listened to my friends talk and laugh as they opened more wine and started up the music. As if perfectly timed, "Girls Just Wanna Have Fun" by Cyndi Lauper was the first song to play.

"Is it even possible to *not* dance to this song?" Leah asked.

"No, not possible," Rachel said as she playfully pulled Maya off the couch. Maya laughed as she joined the others dancing. I noticed a new happiness about her, a lightness that wasn't there before.

"Ladies, my hands are too full of food to fix myself a drink. Will someone help a girl out?"

"I'm on it!" Amber found the pitcher of Loopie's Lemonade and poured a tall glass for me. Then she reached for another kombucha.

Leah asked, "Do you really like that stuff, or are you doing it for health reasons? It reminds me of carbonated vinegar."

Amber took a little taste. "I actually like it. I mean, yeah, some of them can be pretty tart tasting, kinda like a moscato or a lambic, but some can be really sweet, more like a hard cider."

"Minus the buzz! Give me wine over kombucha any day." Leah reached for a bottle of Chardonnay.

Rachel set disposable plates and napkins on the table. "We're going paper tonight."

"As long as we can still have candles," I said as I moved the food onto the table. "A dinner without candles is like dress pants without a belt."

I switched the music to the "Chick Chill" playlist as everyone sat at the table. "Endless Love" by Lionel Richie and Diana Ross started to play.

"Every time I hear this song, I think about Scott Brown," Maya said. "I had such a crush on him. Remember the Sadie Hawkins dance? It took me forever to get up the nerve to ask him to go with me, but when we danced to this song, I was in heaven."

"I think we were all crushing on him. I wonder what he's like now," I said.

"I actually tracked him down on Facebook not too long ago." Maya's voice trailed off.

"Wait. Is he dead?" I immediately jumped to the dramatic.

"Oh, c'mon!" said Maya. "No, he's not dead. But he's definitely not what I remember."

"Why, what's up with him?" Rachel asked.

"I searched for him for years—scoured Facebook, Googled his name, looked at every single 'Scott Brown face' on Google Images that I could bear. Then, I finally found him." She paused. "Umm, he didn't age very well."

"Did any of us age well?" Rachel asked.

"Speak for yourself! I think I'm aging like a fine wine," Maya said with a grin.

"Me too," Leah chimed in. "Fifty is the new thirty, right?"

"Right! But not poor Scott," Maya continued. "From what I can tell from his Facebook posts, he's had some pretty major health issues, and it shows."

"That's too bad. He was such a fox!" I said.

"Total babe," Amber agreed.

"Totally! For sure!" Maya quipped.

We were cracking up, remembering our teenage slang. We spent the rest of dinner using words like bitchin', rad, killer, and cackling over all the Valley Girl slang—totally awesome, like, oh my God! We were definitely California girls.

Our plates now empty, Leah let out a groan. "I'm so full! I feel like I've done nothing but eat all day. We've been grazing like cows. Mooooo."

We all laughed.

"Oh, we're not done yet," I said. "It's not a girls' trip unless you have chocolate and ice cream. I picked up a little something from a local place called Twenty-Four Blackbirds Chocolates." I ducked into the kitchen and came out with a box of thirty-five assorted truffles, Talenti sea salt caramel gelato, and bowls and spoons. "They make the chocolate from scratch."

"Lisa, you're really spoiling us," Maya said. "You're giving me a complex. Remind me to be on my best behavior when you visit me at my bakery. I just know you'll be silently judging me."

"Not a chance. Well, maybe a little, actually," I said with a smirk.

Leah let out a dramatic groan. "Dang it, Lisa! I'm about to burst, but I can't turn down chocolate."

"Well, you'll just have to unbutton those perfectly fitting jeans, won't you?" Maya teased.

As I opened the box, the scent of rich, dark chocolate filled the room. The smell was intoxicating—rich and earthy with hints of vanilla.

"Ohhh, take a big whiff of this," Maya said. "I want my bakery to smell like this."

Rachel picked out a chocolate with a shiny jewel-toned purple coating and took a bite, savoring it. "Oh dang, this is so good!"

We dove into the box like kids on Halloween. Rachel announced she'd found raspberry. Maya discovered a gold-dusted salted caramel. "This is heaven," she moaned.

I tried one with white chocolate drizzle—*passion fruit*, I thought.

Leah took just two chocolates, eating them in careful, tiny bites. A look of discomfort flashed across her face.

"Leah, seriously, are you okay?" I asked. "You look like you're about to birth a food baby."

"Just a little stomachache. I'll be right back." She headed to the bathroom.

The rest of us kept talking, passing around the gelato, not thinking much of it. But time passed—longer than it should have for a quick bathroom break.

"Leah's been in there a while," Rachel said, glancing toward the hallway.

"Maybe everything's *not* coming out okay," Maya joked.

A few more minutes passed. When Leah finally emerged, she seemed to be forcing a smile. Her eyes were slightly red, and her face looked damp, as if she'd splashed cold water on it.

"Did you take a shower in there or something?" Rachel asked.

Leah fanned her face. "Just freshening up!" She sat down and lifted her glass in what looked like a toast. "That chocolate was amazing, Lisa. But at our next get-together, Maya is going to be in charge of desserts."

"Well, you know how I like to plan everything, but I suppose I can let Maya take over desserts." I gave Maya a huge smile.

It got quiet. Maya put her hand over her heart and teared up. "You guys, you have no idea how important your support is to me. I truly don't know if I ever would have considered leaving nursing for real if it weren't for your encouragement."

"We're so excited for you! Another toast—" We all raised our glasses. "To Maya. May you step into a version of yourself you never even dreamed could be so good."

"That's a good wish for all of us," Amber said—but she wasn't looking at us. She was staring at the candle, smiling to herself.

It was quiet for a moment. We all exchanged glances.

"All right, spill it," I said. "We haven't heard much from you over the past few years, and there have been a couple of times on this trip that you've seemed a million miles away. What's going on?"

She watched the candle, its dancing flame reflecting in her eyes. "Sometimes really bad things happen, and you think it's the end of the world. But it's not the end. You just pick up and get back to living life. Even if it looks really different, life still goes on."

"That sounds ominous," Rachel said carefully.

Amber glanced at her, then back at the candle. "Kim picked up the pieces. Maya's dreaming of a brand new future. There's always hope, and that makes me happy." She paused. "I'm … I've just had a lot of changes in my life. I'm starting over in a lot of ways too."

"Changes can be good," Maya said encouragingly.

"Well, we know you stopped cutting hair," Rachel said. "Soooo, I'm guessing that didn't happen because you got bored?"

Amber hesitated. "It's kind of a long story, and you're probably going to be angry with me. I could just really use good friends loving on me right now. I don't want to hurt our friendship."

"How do you know we'll be angry?" Leah asked.

"Because I would be if I heard this story."

"Oh come on, Amber," Maya said, "we're your oldest friends. You think you can lose us that fast?"

"Yeah, but—"

Rachel interrupted her. "Amber, remember in tenth grade when you convinced us to sneak out, and we got caught by the cops?"

"Or that time you dared Lisa to ask out that guy at the mall, and he turned out to be twenty-five?" Leah said.

"Or that time you—"

"Okay, okay, I get it." Amber managed a small smile.

"If those things didn't shake our love for you, what could?" I was trying to be playful, but Amber kept staring at the candle.

"Wait, you're serious," Rachel said. "What did you do? Kill someone?"

"No. But I could have. And you're probably going to want to kill me when I tell you how."

We waited. All the lightheartedness from moments ago had completely evaporated. Now, there was nothing but concern.

Amber's eyes darted around the room. Then she looked down and said, "I got a DUI. With kids in the car."

Stunned silence.

Nobody moved. Nobody spoke. I could hear the fire hissing softly in the background, the ocean outside. My mind was racing—*Amber? Our Amber? Drinking and driving with kids?*

Amber seemed to brace herself for whatever was coming.

We sat there, frozen. Eyes wide. Mouths open.

The seconds stretched out, each one heavier than the last. I didn't know what to say. I didn't know what to think. This was Amber—responsible, careful Amber. The one who always followed the rules, who'd been coached her whole life to be disciplined and structured.

And yet here she was, telling us she'd driven drunk with children in the car.

I looked around at the others. Rachel's face had gone pale. Maya's hand was pressed against her mouth. Leah looked like she might be sick.

Amber sat perfectly still, waiting for one of us to say something. Anything.

The candle flickered between us, indifferent to the bomb that had just been dropped in the room.

Five

"Please tell us you're kidding, Amber." Rachel's voice was quiet, almost pleading. "That doesn't sound like you at all."

"I know. But it happened." She looked back at the candle, unable to meet our eyes. "Are you still interested in all the details now?"

"Of course," I said, trying to shake off the shock. "Let's go to the living room, though, so we can get a little more comfortable."

We all pushed our chairs back, grabbed our glasses, and moved to the couches. The dishes stayed on the table as something much more important had our attention.

We created a circle around Amber, curling up close to give her our full support.

Amber sat up straight and held her knees to her chest. "I've tried to keep this secret from so many people. It feels weird to talk about it, but—"

"It's okay," said Rachel. "Just start from the beginning."

"Whew. Okay. From the beginning. I guess the real beginning starts all the way back in college when I broke my back."

"I can't imagine how hard that must have been for you," Maya said. "In high school, gymnastics was practically your whole life."

"Yeah, it had to be my whole life if I wanted to be competitive. I was always a good athlete, but I also worked harder than everyone else."

"Didn't you get a full ride to compete?" I asked.

"I did. To Oklahoma. And I was really, really good. I thought I was set." Amber got quiet for a minute, and we all waited for her to keep going.

"I loved it, but it was incredibly intense. I got along great with my coach, and she even promised me a spot on her coaching team after graduation. So I got a part-time job coaching twelve-year-old girls at a local gym. The extra money was nice, and honestly, if anyone can teach you to coach, it's a bunch of girls about to hit puberty. They're dramatic and emotional and they question everything you say."

I was glad she could joke about it. What a relief to take a break from the seriousness of the conversation.

"It must have been like herding cats," Leah said. "Very hormonal cats who cried about everything."

Amber agreed. "That's exactly right. Were we that dramatic?"

"Um, yes. Yes, we were," I said. "I remember one girl in our PE class who sobbed for ten minutes because someone said her ponytail looked stupid."

"I think I remember that!" Amber looked away, reflective. She seemed to be preoccupied with her thoughts. Finally, she said, "It was challenging, but I loved my life. I had my whole future laid out. I knew exactly where I was going."

"Tell us about the fall," Maya said.

Amber's face changed. She squinted her eyes, like she was examining a picture of the scene. "I was a senior, and we were at the NCAA Gymnastics Championships. I was doing great. Then I got to the uneven bars—that's one of my strongest events. But this time, I just ... slipped, I guess. I don't remember much about the fall. I remember my left hand sliding off the bar, and I was in the air just long enough to think, *oh shit!* Then I landed. The pain was so sharp I could barely breathe."

"Oh, Amber!" I interrupted.

"I knew it was really bad, but I didn't know yet that I broke my back—a wedge fracture."

"A wedge fracture? Sounds terrible. What is it?" Leah asked.

Maya chimed in. "It's a type of compression fracture. Happens from falling and landing hard at an angle. The front part of a vertebra collapses, but the back doesn't, making a wedge shape. Very painful."

"Yes it is," Amber said. "Needless to say, that was the end of my season. I was grateful that I wasn't paralyzed, but it didn't take too long to figure out that my days of competing—or even doing anything with gymnastics at all—were over, too."

"That had to be devastating," I said. "Must've really messed with your head. Was it too hard to go back and be around it after you couldn't do it anymore?"

"No, it wasn't that so much. I did have some trauma that the school sports psychologist walked me through, and I had no desire to get on the bars again. But it wasn't about the mental stuff. It was the pain that just never went away. I'm still dealing with it today."

"Oh, I think I know where this is going," Maya said, leaning in. "So, what happened?"

"When I first recovered enough to move around, I tried to go back to my coaching job, but even that was too painful. I could barely move. I kept waiting for the pain to get better, but it just wasn't. It was always there as a dull ache, and if I moved too quickly, it would send a sharp stab into my hip. And I was so stiff. I had to move a little bit, but if I moved too much, I would be miserable for the rest of the day."

"You had to find the sweet spot," Rachel said.

"Yeah. And anything to do with gymnastics was out of the sweet spot. I couldn't believe this had happened to me. I eventually had to tell my coach that I couldn't even work anymore."

Tears welled up in Amber's eyes. "That was one of the hardest conversations of my life."

Rachel reached out and touched Amber's knee. "I remember you loved your coach."

"She was amazing. I was graduating, and she saw that I had no clue what I was going to do with my life, so she helped me explore some ideas."

"That's a good coach," Leah said quietly. "When you lose the path you thought you were on, it's so hard to see what else is even possible."

"It really is. I was getting my degree in business management. She asked me what other things I enjoyed doing. I'd always been good at hair, so I decided to go to cosmetology school. I thought maybe I could have my own salon."

"It didn't surprise me that you went into that," I said. "Remember when you did my hair for Senior Ball? I loved how you styled it that night!"

"And you were always helping us color and perm our hair," Leah added.

"Ugh, the hideous perms, with our hair teased up to the sky. We all smelled like Aqua Net." Rachel crinkled her nose. "Thank God hairspray doesn't smell like that anymore!"

"That's the truth." Amber looked wistful again.

"You seemed to love doing hair," I said.

"Oh, I did. And I could totally work my schedule around Emily. It was great that way. When she got into gymnastics, I even became the team mom … I needed that. I missed competing so much. At least I could watch Emily experience it. She's really good, too. I think she'll get a scholarship."

"So what went wrong?" Rachel asked.

"Let me guess," Maya said, watching Amber closely. "The pain. I've seen so much of this at the hospital. This is an addiction thing, isn't it?"

Amber's voice was shaky. "Yes. But not right away. It evolved into something like that."

"Were you on Oxy back then?" Maya asked.

"Yeah, then I took Percocet for quite a while. And that numbed the pain really well, but the side effects were terrible for me. I didn't like how it made me feel—constipated, tired all the time. My stomach was all torn up, and my whole body seemed to hurt even more. So, I eventually stopped taking it and just used anti-inflammatories and ice. I popped Advil like it was candy. That got me by."

"Did your doctor ever suggest anything else?" Leah asked. "Physical therapy or anything?"

"I tried physical therapy for a while, but it was hit or miss. Some days it helped, some days it made things worse.

I just learned to live with it. I stayed busy doing hair, built up my client list … I was actually doing pretty well."

"That's how you and John met, isn't it?" I asked.

"Yep. He came in for a haircut and left with my phone number." Her whole body seemed to relax for the first time since she started sharing her story. "He and Emily are the best things to ever come out of all this mess."

"Ugh," Leah said, "I can't imagine being pregnant with a bad back."

"Yeah, that was tough. I had to be on bed rest for the last trimester, and I had to have her by C-section. After that, I was done trying to have more kids. It was too hard on me."

"But cutting hair all day … was it hard to stand all that time?" Leah asked.

"I had this special stool that I used so I could half sit, half stand, and I was able to keep the pain to a dull ache with the stool. I don't know, it just kind of became my normal. The pain was always there, but I learned to ignore it. I did pilates to try to stay in shape. That helped too.

"But as I got older, my body started wearing down. After years of doing hair, my neck and shoulders started to hurt too, and the sharp pain in my hip came back. And then, going to the gymnastics meets with Emily and sitting on those hard benches … it started to become unbearable."

"Did you get back on painkillers?" Rachel asked.

"No, I didn't want the side effects. But one night, John and I went to dinner after a tough day, and we ordered a glass of wine, then two. That evening, I forgot about the pain for a few hours. It felt so good. The next evening, I had another couple of drinks. And the next, and the next."

"But we all do that," Leah said. "I have a drink almost nightly."

"Yeah, but it's different when you're drinking to relieve pain," Maya said. "And it's terrible medicine for pain. I took a class on this once for my continuing education requirements. Alcohol depresses your nervous system, so your perception of pain is lower, but when the alcohol wears off, your nervous system rebounds and you become super-sensitive. It's called hyperalgesia. So you perceive the pain even more than before you drank, which makes you need to drink again. That rebound keeps getting bigger and bigger, and soon you're drinking more and more just to get the same relief."

Amber was quiet for a moment, processing Maya's words. "Well, Maya just explained what happened, I guess. I was drinking in the evenings, and it seemed like my back was hurting even more during the day. Then I added a drink at lunch to dull that afternoon pain, especially on days when I had to leave work and go straight to one of Emily's events. It really helped me get through the rest of the day.

"But I couldn't just crack one open in front of my clients, so I would pour a little vodka in my Coke or iced tea, followed by a lot of breath mints. It's easy to mix vodka into any drink. I wasn't drinking huge amounts, so it was pretty easy to hide."

"Oh, Amber," I whispered.

Amber choked up a little. "It's hard to admit that I was sneaking alcohol. But I gotta face it. It's not going away.

"Anyway, I started drinking throughout the day. I just kept adding. I didn't mean to, but the minute the pain relief wore off, I started hurting again so bad.

"I guess I built up a tolerance, because I wasn't drunk. Ever. I started to need the alcohol just to feel normal. I just wanted to function like a successful, happy businesswoman and mom."

"Didn't John notice?" I asked. "Not even in the bank account? That had to cost a ton of money. And what did you do with the bottles?"

"I had my own business. I just told him that I had fewer clients than normal, so I wasn't making as much money. And ... oh man, I'm so embarrassed ... I would hide bottles everywhere and then throw the empties away at gas station trash cans.

"I ended up drinking all day long. But I didn't feel drunk. I didn't act drunk. I just felt ... normal." She paused. "And I was driving through it all."

"Were your reactions slower?" Rachel asked.

"Maybe. But not by much. I didn't notice it."

"Why didn't you tell us?" I asked, my voice catching. "Why didn't you get help?"

Amber leaned back, shrinking into the couch. "Because I thought I was managing. I thought I had it under control. And I wasn't fall-down, sloppy drunk. I felt as normal as I do now."

"But obviously you didn't have it all under control," Rachel said, an edge to her voice. "So, what happened?"

Amber's eyes welled up, and a single tear rolled down her face. Maya found a tissue and gave it to Amber. Then she sat back down and leaned in again.

"There was a meet in the next town over. I finished work early so I could take Emily to it. She and two of her teammates got into my car, and we started driving there."

"Was there an accident?" Maya asked.

"Yes, but I swear that I didn't cause it," Amber said, looking at each of us. "We were just getting into town, and a car pulled out from one of the side streets right in front of me. I hesitated. Just for a second. But by the time I reacted, it was too late. It was all so fast—I don't think I could have avoided it, even if I didn't have any alcohol in my system. Anyway, I hit the lady on the driver's side back door. I was able to swerve just enough to miss her directly."

"How were the girls?" Rachel asked. "Did anyone get hurt?"

"No, everyone was okay. Pretty shaken up though.

"Both of our cars were damaged, so we exchanged insurance information and called the police. One of the other parents was on the way to pick the girls up and get them to the meet."

"So how did you get a DUI?" Leah asked.

"The police officer smelled alcohol on my breath. I don't know how—I hadn't been drinking since we got in the car together. And I wasn't the one who caused the accident, but he made me do a field sobriety test. I had to walk the line in front of everyone. I guess I didn't do so well. He pulled out a breathalyzer. I blew a .10."

Amber's hands were shaking. She gripped her tissue tighter, knuckles white.

"That day, sitting in the back of a cruiser in handcuffs, was the first day of my completely sober life."

"Oh God," Leah said, thoughtful. "I've driven after drinking before, thinking that maybe I shouldn't drive. Right on that edge. We all have, haven't we?"

An uncomfortable silence fell over the group.

"I mean, not often," I said. "But yeah. A couple of glasses of wine at dinner and then driving home. Not drunk, but a little buzz. It only takes one cop, one traffic stop ..."

"We've been lucky," Rachel said.

"What happened to the girls when you got arrested?" I asked.

"They waited there by my wrecked car until the other girl's mom arrived to take them." Amber wiped her nose. "You guys, Emily was absolutely mortified. She barely looked at me, and when she did, all I could see was confusion and questions. I had betrayed her."

"What about the other girls?" Maya asked.

"They were just really quiet, but they stayed close to Emily and hooked their arms into hers. I'm glad they were there to comfort her. But when the other mom got there ..." Amber let out a choked laugh. "I think she would have slapped me upside the head if a cop wasn't there. She was beyond mad.

"Looking back on it, I knew I wasn't at my best. But I don't think I ever would have admitted it to myself. I was just managing. Making it all work. But if something had happened to any of those kids ... I don't know how I could have lived with that."

"How could you blow a .10 and not feel drunk?" Leah asked.

"Because she built up a tolerance," Maya explained. "It happens with alcohol abuse. You just don't get the buzz anymore. You feel awful when you withdraw and then drink just to feel normal. But the alcohol still affects your reaction time, even if you don't feel it."

I leaned back on the couch and stared at the ceiling. The fireplace cast flickering shadows across the walls. I could hear the ocean outside, steady and constant.

We all sat in silence for a moment, letting the weight of it sink in.

Maya got up and got Amber a glass of water and some more tissues. Thankful for the break to decompress from the heaviness, we all relaxed back in our seats. Amber wiped her eyes and took a drink of water.

"Okay, how did it all play out?" Rachel asked when we had settled back in.

"Well, that was an adventure," Amber said with heavy sarcasm. "John had to deal with a wrecked car, a devastated daughter, and a drunk wife. He had no clue about what was going on.

"We actually separated for a couple of weeks, but that was even harder on Emily. So, as long as I was totally honest and did everything I could to get help, he said he would try to stick it out with me.

"Everything came out. To everyone. The whole gymnastics team knew. All of Emily's friends knew. Emily went from being embarrassed to being really hurt. Both John and Emily understood why I started drinking and what I was trying to do, but they didn't understand why I kept it all a secret from them."

"So why did you keep it a secret?" I asked.

"What could I say? 'Hey, honey, my back is hurting so bad that I started drinking to help numb the pain, and now I'm drinking pretty much every waking moment, and I can't stop.'"

Amber continued, exasperated, "We're supposed to be strong. And successful. And Wonder Woman. We're not supposed to be too weak to handle our problems. It wasn't supposed to be like this."

"That's such a lie, Amber." Leah's voice was thick with emotion. "It's so easy to get caught up in perfectionism, and it can become such a prison. I deal with this too. But I keep telling myself—and I'll tell you—we're not supposed to be perfect. It's okay to need help."

"We could have helped you walk through this, Amber," I said. "I would have dropped everything and come to you. You know that, right?"

"We all would have," Rachel added.

Amber wiped her eyes. "I know, but I just couldn't risk losing more friends."

"You wouldn't have lost us," I said. "We would have been disappointed, yeah. Maybe even mad. But we would have loved you through it. And sometimes love means telling you hard truths when your vision gets cloudy. When you're too close to see what's really happening. That's what friends do."

"Because we love you," Rachel said. "Even when it's tough."

"You're not the sum of your mistakes, Amber," Maya said. "You're so much more than that. You're an amazing wife, mother, and friend who made a mistake. Your drinking is not all you are."

"Yeah? Tell that to everyone who found out about this. The anger and disappointment were palpable. All the other parents avoided me like the plague. For a long time, they couldn't see past that car accident."

"Is it still like that?" Maya asked.

"No," Amber admitted. "Thankfully, it's slowly changing. I've done a lot of work to rebuild trust with everyone."

"Did you go to court?" Rachel asked.

"Yeah. I didn't get any jail time, thank God. I had to pay a fine and be on probation for six months. The judge ordered me to check into a rehab facility for thirty days and then attend AA meetings three times a week. I also had to do one hundred hours of community service. And I had an ignition interlock device on my car for six months."

"What is that?" Leah asked.

"It's basically a breathalyzer that's attached to the ignition. Every time I wanted to start the car, I had to blow into it. If it detected anything above .01, the car wouldn't start. And when I was driving, I had to blow into it every thirty minutes to keep the car running. I hated doing that in front of people."

"I guess that's one way to rebuild trust with people," Rachel said dryly. "They can see with their own eyes that you're not drinking every time you get in the car."

"Yeah, I guess so," said Amber. "I've had many humbling experiences from all of this."

"Well, every bad thing that happens to us has a silver lining," I said. "What's been the silver lining in all of this?"

For the first time during this conversation, Amber's face softened. "Well, it was a wake-up call. I realized I was slowly destroying myself, and it was time to fix that.

"I had to figure out how to handle the pain. I faced the fact that I couldn't keep doing hair. It was scary to step away, but John supported me. I did my community service at a community center in town, and I really enjoyed working there. When a part-time job opened up, I went for it. It's less money, but I like it, and the part-time hours are easier on my back.

"I also went to a pain management specialist. They implanted a TENS unit in my back—it's this little device that blocks pain through electronic signals. Most of the time, the pain is much more manageable."

"That's amazing," Maya said. "But what happens when the battery runs out?"

"I sleep on a pad that recharges it. It's kind of like a wireless charger for a phone."

Rachel smiled and winked. "You're rechargeable. That's very 2020s of you."

"It's incredible that technology like that exists now," Leah said. "No more constant pain?"

"Not constant, no. It really helps me a lot."

"That's so cool. What else is in your silver lining?" I asked.

Amber thought for a moment. "With all the counseling, John, Emily, and I are closer than I think we've ever been. We were just so busy doing life, and this whole thing made us slow down and start digging a little deeper, ya know? John and I have started going on regular dates and working on our marriage. I think we've fallen in love all over again."

"That's beautiful," Leah said.

"And I've never stopped going to AA meetings. I've been working hard on the 'making amends' step—to my family and to the other gymnastics families. They're actually being really cool to me now because they see me working hard to stay sober. I even got invited recently to speak at Emily's school about my story."

"That's amazing!" Rachel said. "I'm so proud of you, Amber. You'll really be able to connect with those kids when you tell them your story. When are you going to do it?"

"I haven't said yes yet. I don't know if I'm ready for that. But last month, I got my two-year coin! Through the 12-step program, we are rewarded with coins to mark sobriety. It sounds kinda corny, but I am so proud when I receive them."

We all erupted.

"Two years!"

"Amber, that's incredible!"

"We need to celebrate that—"

But as Leah said it, we all looked at each other, the same thought occurring to us at once.

"Amber, that's so wonderful. Congratulations," I said, my voice softening. "And, I'm just realizing that we've been drinking in front of you all weekend. What is this doing to you?"

"Oh my goodness, yes," Rachel said. "We're so sorry."

Amber thought for a moment, then grinned. "I'm handling it. The only time I struggled was Friday night. Remember when I stepped outside and was on the phone for about twenty minutes?"

"Yes, and we were teasing you pretty hard about talking on the phone instead of being with us," I said.

"I had been preparing myself all weekend to deal with being around booze. When the alcohol first came out, I started to have a little pity party for myself. We always had so much fun when we were drinking together. I was missing that feeling. I hated the fact that I couldn't just do whatever I wanted.

"So, I called my sponsor to talk through it. She's amazing—you guys would adore her. Anyway, she let me process it with her, and I realized that drinking with you guys was never going to give me back the feeling of fun that I was missing. That's just not why I drink anymore. Alcohol has a different purpose for me, and that doesn't change just because I'm with you. Once I worked through that, I was totally okay.

"So no, it doesn't bother me to see you girls drink. I don't need the alcohol to have fun with you. Besides, I'm not giving up my two-year coin for anyone. Not even you guys!"

"That right there," Leah said, pointing at Amber, "that's strength. That's where you're the real Wonder Woman."

Amber looked at us nervously. "So, you really aren't mad at me?"

"I'm a little upset that you didn't let us walk through this with you," I said. "But like we said, you're so much more than your mistakes."

Amber's shoulders dropped. She seemed relieved.

"Man, I don't think I was breathing at all when I was telling you about it."

"I don't think we were either," Rachel said. "Let's all take a couple of breaths."

Everyone breathed in deep at the same time, which sent us into a laughing fit. We could feel the tension drain from the room.

"Well, you're right, Amber. That was a doozy," Maya said. "I didn't have that on my Santa Barbara trip bingo card!"

"Seriously, though, you look really peaceful," I said. "It's like you're more present with us now."

Amber thought for a moment. "I guess I didn't realize how much mental weight I was carrying by not telling you guys. But I'm glad I finally did. The shame of it all felt like a monster on my back. But it seems like the more I talk about it—name it—the less power it has over me."

"What's that saying? Something like, you're only as sick as your secrets?" asked Leah.

"We say that in AA all the time. It really does feel true. I feel better. Stronger." Amber leaned forward and stretched her arms out. "You know, I think that I even feel a little better physically."

"That doesn't surprise me at all," Maya said. "So many illnesses are caused by stress. I think our bodies actually have a chance to heal when we're not carrying all that mental baggage around."

Amber looked at each of us gathered around her, supporting her, loving her. Her eyes filled with tears again, but this time, they were tears of gratitude.

"Thank you for still loving me. For being a safe place for me to talk about this. I was so afraid of your disappointment. But instead, I feel ... I don't know, I feel a little more free."

"Amber, there's nothing you could do that would make us stop loving you," I said. "And we might have said some tough things that you didn't want to hear, but tough love is still love."

"Sometimes, the only way *out* of a tough situation is *through*," Rachel said. "And you're doing it. And now we get to celebrate every win with you. We're so proud of you."

We pulled Amber into a group hug. More tears, but good ones this time.

Almost as if it was scripted, "Count On Me" by Lucy Schwartz started playing.

"I freaking *love* this song!" I said. "It's from my favorite movie … *The Women*. This should be our theme song, Chickies!"

"Whoa," said Maya, "Now that I'm standing up, my bladder is about to explode!" She called back, mid-rush to the bathroom, "And yes, I love that movie too, Lisa!"

"I've got the downstairs bathroom!" Rachel's voice rang out. "The rest of you can line up after me!"

After a bathroom break, we cleaned up the kitchen and then headed back to the couches. We sat for a while longer, drinking, talking, processing. The weight of Amber's story hung in the air—not heavy with judgment, but with love.

Finally, Amber yawned. Then Rachel.

"It's late," I said, glancing at my phone. "We should probably get to bed."

"I don't want to," Maya said. "Part of me wants to keep packing in every minute I can with you guys. This weekend is almost over."

"Then we'll just have to do this more often," Rachel said firmly.

We gathered our glasses and cleaned up the living room.

Rachel said, "Those two bathrooms are about to get quite the workout. We're all going to be fighting for mirror space."

Maya looked at Leah. "What do you think? One more drink? I'm still pretty wound up."

Leah picked up the wine bottle. "We'll have one more while you guys go ahead and get ready for bed. That way, the bathrooms won't turn into a battle zone."

"Good idea," I said. "I'll turn off most of the lights so you won't have to. Much more relaxing anyway."

I switched off the overhead lights, leaving just the small lamp on the side table glowing softly. The gas fireplace was still on, its flames dancing behind the glass, casting a warm, flickering light across the living room.

"Night, you two," Rachel said, heading toward the stairs.

Giving Maya's shoulder a little squeeze as she passed, Amber said, "Don't stay up too late."

"We won't," Maya promised.

Leah and Maya settled onto the couch as the rest of us headed for bed. Maya poured each of them a small glass of wine.

Downstairs, there was a flurry of activity in the bathrooms—brushing teeth, washing faces, putting on pajamas. Rachel and Amber went into their room and closed the door. They were chattering and giggling like a couple of girls jumping into their bunk beds at summer camp.

I climbed into my bed, pulled the covers up, and reached for my phone to set my alarm.

My phone wasn't on the nightstand.

I sat up, looking around. Not on the dresser. Not plugged in anywhere. Then I remembered—I'd left it upstairs on the kitchen counter when I was cleaning up after dinner.

I sighed and slipped out of bed as quietly as I could. I tiptoed out of the room and started up the stairs, being careful to avoid the creaky spots I'd discovered over the weekend.

As I reached the top of the stairs, I heard Maya say, "Can I talk to you about something?"

I froze, still hidden in the stairwell.

Leah and Maya were sitting on the couch. I could just see the top of Maya's blonde ponytail over the back of the cushions.

I should announce myself. Just walk in, grab my phone, say, "Sorry, forgot this," and head back downstairs.

That's what I should do.

But my feet wouldn't move.

Shame on me, I thought. *I should just mind my own business and go back to bed.*

But who was I kidding? This was clearly going to be important. Maya and Leah had always had a special bond, and the vulnerability I heard in Maya's voice made me want to understand what was happening.

I stayed perfectly still at the top of the stairs, hidden in the shadows, trying to remain invisible.

Six

"Of course. What's up?"

Leah was sitting just out of view. The room was quiet except for the soft hiss of the gas fireplace. Shifting shadows from the fire danced across the walls. The lamp on the side table glowed warm and low.

I could see Maya's ponytail turn to face Leah. Even from a distance, I could feel sudden tension in the room.

"When you came out of the bathroom tonight, your face was red and blotchy," Maya said carefully. "And you looked shaky. And when I went in after you later on ..." She paused. "I saw the wet rags by the sink. The paper towels in the trash. Leah, are you okay?"

Silence.

"I'm fine," Leah said, her voice curt.

"Leah, I remember back in high school. The bulimia. Has it started up—?"

Leah cut her off. "I said I'm fine. Can we just drop it? The last thing I need is for my friend to tell me what a loser I am."

"I would never think that about you, Leah. Look, I'm not criticizing you. I'm not judging you. But I know what I saw, and I love you too much to let tonight go by without saying anything."

Oh, Leah, I thought from my hiding spot, tucked behind the wall. My heart hurt for her. I had no idea.

The room was quiet for a moment. The downstairs heat turned on, and a gentle current of air started to flow up the stairs and into the living room.

"Leah, you know I love you. We've been friends since we were twelve. We were best friends back then. And yeah, we don't see each other as much anymore, but you're still one of my people. I'm not going anywhere. Please just talk to me."

There was a sniffle, and then I could hear Maya stand up and get some napkins from the table. Then she took her place again on the couch.

Leah sighed, then blew her nose. "I started to do it. But then I stopped. I was afraid I wouldn't be quiet enough. So, I had a bit of a cry and then washed my face with cold water. That's why I looked like that."

"Oh, Leah, why haven't you told me?"

Leah sounded choked up. "I can't believe I'm still dealing with this. It's so embarrassing. How stupid am I that I still can't shake this? Please, Maya, please don't tell the others."

"Of course not. I've never told anyone. Not once. And I won't now. And you're not stupid. Now, can we please talk about it? What happened tonight?"

Leah took a moment before responding. "I guess I was feeling overwhelmed. It's so good to be back with the gang again. Kinda like old times. But I had a lot of bad memories from back then, and, well … some of them started popping back up."

"I noticed you were pretty anxious about the food tonight."

"Yeah, that triggered me a little bit. I'm just really structured with my eating, and it seemed like we had grazed all day long."

"I get that." Maya's voice was faint.

I imagined Leah setting her water on the table when I heard a clink in the silence.

"You've always been my safe place, Maya. You know that, right? You're the only one who really knows about my family. About how bad it was. And you never pushed me for too many details. I was living it. I sure didn't want to talk about it."

"You know what I remember, Leah? You'd show up at my house with your backpack and just … stay. For days sometimes."

"Yeah, I basically lived at your house when we weren't in school. I couldn't breathe in my own house. It was a war zone."

"What would set them off?"

"Everything. Nothing. My dad was drunk more than he was sober. And when he was home, he was yelling. Usually at my mom, sometimes at me. It was always so loud at my house. It was a relief when he'd leave the house to go out drinking."

"I remember you saying that once. That you were happier when he wasn't there."

"Yeah, at least then it was just my mom. But she ..." Leah searched for the words. "She was such a narcissist. God, she was so critical, Maya. Nothing I did was good enough. I had to be thin, pretty, polished, perfect. Straight A's. The right friends—the thin and pretty and successful ones. Everything about our precious little family had to look perfect on the outside."

"Oh, yeah. She was definitely obsessed with appearances."

"Completely. If I did things right according to her standards, she'd lay off me a little. But if I gained a pound or got a B or wore the wrong thing ..." She trailed off. "The things she'd say to me."

"Like what?" Maya asked.

"That I wasn't pretty enough. Not thin enough. Not good enough. That I was lazy, or stupid, or that I embarrassed her. She was relentless," Leah said, her voice breaking a little. "I had to do everything perfectly just to get her to shut up."

"I get it now. You've always been a perfectionist. I knew it had to do with your home life, but it was actually a matter of survival for you, wasn't it?"

"Yep. And that's why I stayed with you every chance I could. Man, I was so thankful for you and your parents."

I could hear the warmth in Maya's voice. "You were like another daughter to them … and Mom was concerned about your health, too. She suspected you were throwing up. She talked to me about it."

"I'm so glad she didn't say anything to me. I would have been mortified."

The heater shut off. The house was so quiet without that little bit of noise.

Leah wiped her nose as she talked. "Your house was like a refuge. Your parents never yelled or told me everything that was wrong with me. And they were so … happy. I loved that about them."

"So, the bulimia was a way to stay thin? Or a coping mechanism?"

"Both. But you know what I finally figured out in therapy? Disordered eating is more about control than about weight."

"Really?"

"I felt so out of control with everything—my dad, my mom, my life. But my body was mine. What I ate … what I got rid of. It was something they couldn't touch. Even when everything else was falling apart, I had that. Sounds gross, but it was something I could control. Or, at least, I thought I was in control. Turns out, not so much."

"Yeah, I thought you kicked it in college. You sure started looking healthier. Were you still doing it though?"

"I did get better once I got out of the house and away from them. I decided that I was going to be so successful that I'd never have to depend on them for anything ever again. That helped me feel like I was taking my life back.

"In college, I worked with a dietitian and got some counseling. They helped me find some other ways to cope. Journaling helped me the most—it was like older Leah sitting down with younger Leah and just listening, helping her work through the feelings. I still journal almost every day."

"But obviously, you're not completely free."

"This is embarrassing, but no, I still have issues. I'm mostly over it. But when I get really stressed, my mind goes there first. And, I'm ashamed to say it, but I passed this nasty habit on to my daughter."

"Hannah? She does it too?"

"Yep. Turns out she's a chip right off the old block. In so many ways … I feel so bad, Maya. I wouldn't wish it on anybody, and here I am, influencing one of the most important people in my life."

"So, what happened?"

I heard Leah unfold a fresh napkin. "When Hannah was little, I thought I had it under control. I didn't do it very much, but when I did ... I didn't know this, but she witnessed it a few times. The whole nasty mess from beginning to end."

"How did you find out?"

"I was at Hannah's house last year. The toilet wasn't working right in the guest bathroom, so I went to the master bathroom. I saw the rags. It looked exactly like my bathroom. My heart just shattered."

"What did you do?"

"I confronted her, and she admitted it. Then she told me she had seen me do it when she was younger. She said she doesn't do it often and has it under control. Then she didn't want to talk about it anymore.

"The whole conversation was so painful. I hate confrontation. And then to find out that she had witnessed me doing it myself ... I told her I wanted to help her stop, but she just laughed at me and said, 'Mom, really? How are *you* going to *help* me?'"

Maya sat quietly, absorbing the story. The fire flickered gently, coaxing them to keep going.

"How old is Hannah now?"

"Twenty-eight. Successful, workaholic, personal trainer, social media influencer—and bulimic."

"Does she like doing social media?" Maya asked.

"She loves it. Her following has gotten big enough for her to make it her full-time job."

"So, is it stressful? I mean, she looks like the picture of perfect health. And she radiates so much confidence. I never would have guessed … But then again, I wouldn't have guessed it about you either."

"That's the good part of social media. Then there's the bad part. Trolls. And they are so, so bad. My heart just breaks for her. When I get criticized on social media, it's usually my work that gets torn apart. But her critics are tearing her body down. Every little bulge, every dimple, every hair out of place. And there are so many nasty, awful people who are dropping their opinions. I would never be able to deal with that kind of pressure."

"There's probably a lot of jealousy coming her way. She's so beautiful."

"Probably. But it doesn't matter. Words still hurt. And I handed down a terrible way to cope. How pathetic is that?"

Maya sighed. I could see the top of her head tilt up as she looked at the ceiling. "Leah, we're older now. We've both seen a few things and learned some stuff. Can I make an observation?"

"Okay …" Leah's voice sounded wary.

"Back when we were in high school, there was one thing you swore you'd never do. You said it often. Do you remember what it was?"

"Yeah. I swore I'd never be like my parents."

Maya said, "But the verbal beatdown you keep giving yourself ... that's the one way you're still like them."

"What are you talking about?" Leah sounded defiant. "I'm nothing like them. I don't treat people like they did."

"Not others. But listen to how you've been talking about yourself tonight."

Maya's voice was gentle but firm. "Pathetic. Loser. Ashamed. Embarrassed. Stupid. You've been criticizing yourself this entire conversation ... You don't need your parents around to abuse you anymore, Leah. You're doing it to yourself."

The silence made me wonder if I was having trouble hearing, but I eventually heard Leah's voice.

"Well ... that ... landed hard."

"Leah, you're still living in the prison you worked so hard to escape from."

Leah's voice rose as she said, "Oh my gosh, you're right. I am so hard on myself. All the time. I don't mean to be like that!"

"Leah, you gotta let it go. The criticism, the perfectionism ... you gotta decide they're not part of your package anymore. Life is messy—it's a lot of things, but it will never be perfect. Stop trying to make it something that it's not supposed to be."

Leah choked back a sob. "But what will people think of me if I'm not at least trying for perfection?"

"They won't think anything different from what they already do. They love you because you're uniquely you, not because you're perfect. Think about it. Am I perfect?"

"No."

"Do you love me less because of that?"

Leah sniffed. "No."

"Sooooo ..." Maya's voice trailed off.

After letting out what sounded like a nervous laugh, Leah said, "Maya? When did you get so smart?"

I could imagine Maya's signature wink as I heard the click of her tongue. "I went to the School of Hard Knocks, baby."

"I'm dehydrated after all these tears," Leah joked. I heard her stand up, walk to the kitchen for a glass of water, and come back to the couch. The clink on the coffee table let me know she was settling in for more conversation.

The faint rhythmic crash of the waves along the shore was the only sound in the room. I was afraid to move even an inch.

"So," Maya finally said, "what does life look like tomorrow? What are you going to do differently?"

"I don't know ... I think I just need to learn how to let it go. Stop picking everything apart, stop replaying all the ways I get it wrong. Maybe actually look for the good for once."

It got quiet again as Maya waited for Leah to finish her thought.

"And be thankful. I'm going to try to be thankful."

"I love that ... and I'm going to hold you to it. Old habits are hard to break—it's going to feel weird at first. But you've got this."

"God, I hope so." Leah smiled. "I guess that's the whole thing, isn't it? Keep doing it until it stops feeling like I'm faking it."

"Hey, you're allowed to be a work in progress, you know. Just be as patient with yourself as you'd be with someone else."

I imagined both girls sitting there, relaxed, watching the fire. After a few minutes, Leah said, "Maya, thanks for calling me out. I needed it."

"I didn't call you *out*, Leah. I called you *up*. I wasn't trying to tear you down. I just needed to remind you about who you really are."

Leah yawned. "What's the phrase? Iron sharpens iron? Well, I'm glad you did."

"That's what friends are for."

"And … if I kick bulimia for good, maybe I can help Hannah. You know … call her up, like you did with me. Do a little iron sharpening myself."

"So when did *you* get so smart?" Maya teased.

"Tonight, actually!"

That made them giggle, and the more they tried to stop, the louder they got. Every last drop of emotion began to leak out. They squeaked out "Shhhhh" and a muffled "I can't breathe" before another round of giggles set in.

I held my hand over my mouth. It was everything I could do not to be heard as I laughed with them.

Finally, with their energy spent, they both let out a deep sigh laced with the last traces of laughter.

Leah said, "Man, I needed this."

"Me too," Maya replied.

I heard the couch creak as they stood up.

Oh no!

They were going to come downstairs. And here I was, standing at the top of the stairs like some kind of creep.

I moved as quickly and quietly as I could, softly stepping back down the stairs in my bare feet, praying none of the steps would creak. My heart was pounding.

I made it to the bottom just as I heard their footsteps above.

"I'm going to sleep well tonight," Leah said, her voice getting closer.

"I hope I get a good sleep. I'm actually pretty tipsy tonight."

I slipped into my bedroom and quietly closed the door, leaving it open just a crack. I heard them go back and forth between the bedroom and bathroom. Doors latching, water running.

A few minutes later, there was a sound of soft giggles moving down the hallway as they headed to their room. Once the door closed, I snuck back upstairs, grabbed my phone and a glass of water, then went back to bed.

I curled up under the covers, thinking about all I had just heard. I promised myself I would never let them know that I had been listening to every word they said.

With a full heart, I rolled over, already feeling myself slip into sleep.

Leah was on her way.

Seven

I woke before the sun, my mind already buzzing. The house was quiet—just the soft sound of the ocean through the open window and the occasional creak of the Airbnb settling.

I slipped out of bed carefully, not wanting to wake the girls, and tiptoed to the kitchen. Cooking has always been my therapy, my way of showing love. And right now, keeping my hands busy meant I didn't have to think too much about the week I'd just had in Sacramento. About my mom. About the fact that I'd barely let myself grieve.

I pulled open the fridge and started pulling out leftovers—cheese, vegetables, a few eggs. Omelettes. Perfect.

I started heating a pot of water for my fresh cup of Earl Grey. With a beehive portion of honey, of course, my morning would be all set.

I turned the oven on to keep the food warm until everyone got up. As I started chopping vegetables, I heard soft footsteps behind me.

"Morning," Rachel said, her voice still scratchy with sleep.

I turned to greet her. "Morning! You're up early."

"Couldn't sleep. I had the worst night sweats, and I woke up completely soaked. That's such a gross feeling. And my shoulder is bothering me."

Rachel looked at the empty coffee pot. "What, no coffee?"

For just a moment, I winced. *Of course, Lisa has to make it. Lisa always does it.* But then I stopped myself and relaxed. People expected me to do everything because, well, I actually insisted on doing everything. I trained them to think that way.

"I was just getting to that, but you beat me. Have a seat, and I'll get it going for you. Fresh, hot coffee coming up!"

I poured hot water into my cup and dropped a tea bag in to steep. Then I started the coffee. Within minutes, the rich, earthy aroma filled the kitchen.

Rachel inhaled deeply. "That smells wonderful!" She made her way to my side of the counter and pulled a mug from the cabinet. "Lisa, do you not like coffee?"

"Eh, it's complicated. When I was growing up, Edna drank a pot of coffee before noon each day, so the smell of coffee always takes me back to our kitchen. And you know me, I love being in the kitchen! But I can't stand the taste of coffee. I think it's because when Edna was cleaning up after lunch, she would empty her ashtray into the used coffee filter. Now, when I smell coffee, I can't help but associate it with the smell of cigarettes."

Rachel made a face.

"Yuck, right?! By the time I was seven, I had developed a love for hot tea with honey because that's what my Aunt Patti drank, and I liked pretty much anything she liked. I wanted to be just like her."

Rachel poured herself a cup of coffee and leaned against the counter, wrapping both hands around the mug. "Lisa, do you ever sleep? You're always the one doing everything for everyone else. Even in junior high and high school, we'd all be sitting around, and you'd be in the kitchen cooking or cleaning or planning the next thing."

I shrugged, whisking eggs. "I really love doing it. I don't like to just sit. And I guess ..." I paused, trying to find the words. "My mom trained me to take care of everyone. It started by working alongside her in restaurants as her bus girl. Everything had to be perfect. I learned the lesson well." The words came out more sharply than I had intended. "Besides, keeping busy is good for me right now. Keeps me from thinking too much."

She looked pensive as she took another sip of her coffee.

I changed the subject. "Rachel, you look a little tired. How are you feeling this morning?"

She gently rotated her right shoulder. "I'm fine. Just didn't sleep great. I have some chronic shoulder pain from the surgery and treatment. It flares up sometimes."

"Tell me about it—how has your recovery been?"

"It's weird, you know? I look better on the outside—my hair's growing back, I'm not green from chemo anymore. But I still have limitations. Lingering stuff that nobody can see."

"Like what?"

"Nerve sensitivity from the chemo. My hands and feet tingle sometimes. And the fatigue ..." She shook her head. "Some days I feel great. Other days, I can barely get out of bed."

My heart squeezed. "Rachel, I can totally relate to that. You know I've had Lyme disease for twenty-seven years now, right?"

"Yeah. I was so glad when you finally got a diagnosis."

"It was sixteen years before they could figure it out. The severe fatigue, the brain fog, a million symptoms that could've been a bunch of other things. I remember getting up just long enough to get the kids up and off to school, then I'd just plop down in the chair and not move for the next six hours. I just couldn't do it. Now I know what it is, but as I treat it and my body detoxes, I start herxing."

"Herxing? What's that?"

"It's a term named after Dr. Herxheimer. Herxing is a reaction to the meds killing off the bacteria of Lyme disease. It's just like chemo killing off the cancer. You take medicine, and the toxins die off and are released into your bloodstream, and they make you sicker. So it's very bittersweet. You feel super sick, but you know you're getting better."

Rachel's eyes widened. "That sounds exactly like what I've been going through since I ended chemo. I'll be feeling pretty good, and then all of a sudden I'll have days of fever, chills, headaches. I get nauseous and dizzy. And it feels like every muscle in my body hurts."

"Yep. That's herxing. Has it happened often?"

Rachel slumped a little and rested her head on her hand. "Enough that I decided it was time to retire. I couldn't do my job well and fight cancer at the same time." Her eyes softened. "I miss my work. Thank God for Rick, though. I don't know how I would get through it without him."

"Sounds like we both hit the jackpot in the husband category."

"Yeah, I guess Pete has to be incredibly supportive if he's gone through that with you for twenty-seven years."

"Absolutely. Especially now that I actually have a diagnosis. It was hard at first—I was sick without a label. Nobody knew what was wrong or how to fix it." I felt the old frustration starting to rise. "It made me feel so alone because nobody could understand what was happening. I didn't even understand it myself. I thought I was going insane."

I flipped an omelette in the pan. "It can be really difficult for Pete and the kids. It's even affected my hearing. One day, I had normal hearing, and the next day, I could barely hear at all. They never knew what to do for me. They didn't know when to help or when to leave me alone."

"Rick's only had to deal with my medical stuff for a couple of years," said Rachel, "but he's been absolutely amazing. He's taken on so much extra when I have my down days—either because I'm in too much pain or just too fatigued. And my daughters took turns sitting with me through chemo appointments and helping Rick take care of the house. I'm so grateful they live close by.

"Some days I feel really good, and other days I can barely get out of bed and get to the bathroom. But they're always there for me."

"That's so great that your kids live close and can help out." I plated the first omelette, put it in the warm oven, and started on the second. "What about your friends?"

Rachel pursed her lips and shrugged. "Friends are kind of iffy. Most of my friends were through work, so when I retired, I just didn't see them anymore. I think maybe they don't know what to do around me. They know I miss the school. So do they talk about it, or do they avoid the subject altogether? They never just ask me." She took another sip of coffee. "It's been kind of awkward. And I think most people don't understand what's happening because I look decent, but I still have bad days. I think it's easier for them to just stay away."

"What about strangers?" I asked.

Rachel let out a bitter laugh. "Ugh, don't get me started. Most people have very little patience for someone who looks fine but is moving a little slower. I have a handicapped tag to hang on my rearview mirror on rough days, but I get so many dirty looks. Someone actually had the balls to say to me, 'You don't look handicapped to me.' Like they caught me doing something immoral."

She paused and bit her lip. "People don't know how much that hurts."

I could feel that down to my bones. I turned from the stove and looked her in the eyes. "Rachel, I totally get you, and I'm so sorry you have to go through that. We're both living it. Our bodies don't do what they're told to do. You look good on the outside, but you feel like crap on the inside. It sucks when you're quietly struggling just to be normal again. And people don't know what to do with that. They just label it as drama and try to stay away."

Rachel teared up. "You really do get it, don't you?"

I nodded.

"It's a lonely place, isn't it?" she asked. "But I'm really not alone."

"No, I'm right there with you," I replied as I plated up another omelette and popped it in the oven. "And I'll tell you what ... you always have me to talk to. I really get it. And you can hop on a Marco Polo with me any time you want and just let it all out. Sometimes it just feels good to vent to another misfit. We need to stick together."

Rachel gave a wide grin. "Deal. And the same goes for you." She raised her coffee mug. "I guess we're part of a club we didn't ask to be in."

"What club?" Amber asked as she walked into the kitchen.

"Well, good morning," I said, turning back to the stove. "How did you sleep?"

"Better than Rachel, I think," Amber said as she poured herself a cup of coffee.

"Did I keep you up?" Rachel asked.

"Not really. But every time I woke up to use the bathroom or get water, you seemed to either be awake or really tossing and turning. Did you get any sleep?"

"I did. My shoulder was bothering me, but that's been kind of normal since the cancer."

"So what's the club?" Amber asked again.

Rachel and I exchanged looks. "We should come up with a name for it, Rach." I turned to Amber. "We were just talking about the random symptoms that seem to pop up at unpredictable times. We look pretty good on the outside, but we both deal with weird things that nobody else can see."

Maya shuffled into the kitchen just then. "Something smells good," she said, rubbing her eyes. Her long blonde hair was pulled into a messy ponytail.

"Are you awake, Maya?" I asked, laughing. "Rough night?"

"I may have had one too many glasses of wine. And then Leah and I stayed up talking last night. Morning came pretty fast."

"Where is Leah?" Rachel asked.

"Present and accounted for," Leah answered as she walked into the kitchen. She was already dressed in a crisp white linen button-down tucked into tailored khaki shorts. Her light brown hair was pulled back in a sleek, low ponytail. She had already put her makeup on.

"Look at you, up and ready to conquer the world even before breakfast," Amber said.

"I was thinking about taking a walk on the beach before we have to leave," Leah said. "Anyone else up for it?"

"I'm in," Rachel said.

"That sounds great," Maya added.

"Let's do it," Amber agreed.

"Great minds think alike!" I said. "I was hoping we'd do something like that, so I contacted the host—they let me extend our checkout until noon. So let's have breakfast, and then we can take a little time and walk off our meal on the beach."

"Ah, the sign of a well-traveled woman," Rachel said. "Always extend the checkout."

As I finished cooking the omelettes, I put Maya to work cutting fruit. Rachel was in charge of making fresh coffee, and Amber and Leah set the table.

"What, Lisa, no music?" Maya teased.

"Do you actually think I would be without music?" I had been waiting for everyone to wake up. I grabbed my phone and pulled up my "Smooth Jazz" playlist.

"You should know better by now, Maya," Leah said. "Lisa has every little detail planned out. Nice choice of music!"

"If there's one thing Edna taught me, it was how to serve," I said. "Everything with her had to be perfect, down to the tiniest detail. And music is a detail I have always loved to plan."

David Sanborn's saxophone filled the kitchen as we moved the food to the table and sat down. The morning light streamed through the windows, catching the steam rising from our coffee cups.

"Now," Amber said as she took an omelette and passed the plate to Leah, "you and Rachel were talking about weird symptoms that nobody knows about. Lisa, I'm assuming you're talking about Lyme disease?"

"Yeah. I've got a whole laundry list. Brain fog so bad I forget what I'm saying mid-sentence. Joint pain that moves around my body like it's playing hopscotch. Some days I wake up and my hands are so stiff I can barely open them."

I took a sip of my tea. "And this is weird: I lost hearing in my left ear because—well, we think it was because of Lyme disease. So I have a really hard time hearing, especially when you're talking behind me on my left side. And if I'm tired or dehydrated, the ringing in my ear gets so loud that it blocks out everything else. It's so annoying."

"And here I thought you were just choosing to ignore us sometimes," Leah said, grinning.

"I'd never ignore you!" I said, smiling. "Honestly, though, it's difficult when I'm around multiple people. I feel out of place sometimes because I can't hear well, and it's frustrating for people to have to repeat themselves. It's also hard for me to focus on what they're saying. It makes my head spin."

Amber's eyes lit up, like a lightbulb going on in her head. "Is that why you always insist we talk on Marco Polo?"

"Yes! I love Marco Polo or Zoom because that way I can see your face, which helps me understand what you're saying better. I can put the tone and facial expressions and the sound all together."

"Oh, that makes so much sense," Maya said.

"So what about you, Rach?" Amber asked.

Rachel set down her fork. "Now that I look a little more normal and my hair is growing back, it's mostly hidden stuff. Shoulder pain on my right side. Some swelling from lymphedema—my arm gets puffy sometimes. Nausea that comes out of nowhere. And neuropathy in my hands and feet from the chemo. Sometimes they just tingle and go numb."

"There have been so many changes in your body." Maya set down her coffee mug.

"Yes, there have. The first changes were obvious—losing a boob, the chemo side effects."

"I can't imagine what that must have been like," Leah said.

"It was tough for a while. I lost so much of what makes us feel like women ... the hair, the eyelashes and eyebrows, one of my lady lumps ... I just felt like someone had dropped me and tried to put me back together ... but forgot a bunch of parts.

"And seeing myself naked after all that ... I was completely lopsided. Lisa, maybe that's the name of our club. The Lopsided Club. You have only one usable ear, I have only one boob ..."

"Or maybe the One-Off Club," I said with a wink.

While we were making fun of ourselves, Maya was studying her food. She looked up at Rachel. "But seriously, that had to be devastating."

"It was at first. But at the time, I was fighting for my life, so I kinda had bigger things to deal with, ya know?"

"Yeah," said Maya. "It just seems so … I don't know. Dramatic? That's a big change."

"Oh, it was," said Rachel. "But the most dramatic change was going into menopause in a single day."

"What?" we all said at once.

"Rachel," I said, "that sounds awful!"

"Oh yeah. Didn't I tell you about that part? The type of cancer I had feeds on estrogen, so I get a shot every three months that stops my ovaries from making it. So I went from normal perimenopause to full-on hormone shutdown essentially in a day."

"Ohhhhhh," we all groaned in unison.

"I'm in perimenopause right now," Maya said, "and the symptoms are driving me crazy. I can't imagine 'the change' happening overnight."

"Yeah, that was a trip. The hot flashes were relentless," Rachel explained. "I was still working, and I would get hot flashes at the worst times. Once, I was talking to the whole school at an assembly when sweat suddenly started dripping down my face, which was the color of a very ripe tomato. That confused the heck out of those poor kids."

We laughed, thinking about a bunch of kids who hadn't even experienced puberty yet, trying to figure out what was wrong with their principal.

"I've been getting a lot of hot flashes lately," I said. "And for some reason, I usually have a really major one in front of the mirror as I'm putting on my eyelashes and getting ready to go out for dinner with Pete. I'm in a full-out sweat where I have to lie naked on the bed with a fan going. Then I have to get up and get ready all over again."

"Oh, girl!" Rachel started cracking up. "Try doing that in front of a school full of tweens. Taking off my clothes was not an option, obviously."

"Yeah, that would be bad," joked Amber.

Rachel lit up. "That first Halloween, I dressed up in a superhero costume and called myself 'The Hot Flash.'"

"That's hilarious!" said Amber. "Did Rick play along too?"

"Oh yes. He went as 'Captain Clueless' with a big question mark on his chest. He was the husband who had no idea what was happening but was trying his best."

"Wow," said Leah. "He seems like a really great guy."

"Yeah, Rick is my superhero after all of this," Rachel said. "He took it all so well, thank God. Here I was, missing a boob and all scarred up, no hair, sick from chemo ... I couldn't stand to look at myself. But he just acted like I was as beautiful as ever."

"Aww, that's so great that you had that kind of support," Maya said.

"Yeah, and he even still wanted sex! Of course, that's a whole different monster when it comes to menopause. I come to bed all lopsided, feeling half like a guy, holding the biggest bottle of lube you've ever seen in your life, looking at him and saying, 'So, you want some of this?'"

We all started laughing hysterically.

"What does he say?" Leah asked, wiping away tears.

"Um, duh. He's a guy. The bar isn't set real high. I'm alive at this point, and that's pretty much good enough."

More laughter.

"Sex hormones are so wasted on young people," Rachel said. "Sex was just getting really good for me in my forties, and then suddenly all those hormones changed, and now it's the Sahara Desert. But his sex drive is as strong as ever. I think God must have a sense of humor."

"Ugh, I know," I said. "For me, it's like putting a pickle on sandpaper—"

Maya spit out the coffee she had just taken a drink of. "Coffee up my nose ... it burns ... not good," she managed to sputter out as she buried her face in her napkin.

We were howling. Our stomachs hurt and tears were streaming down our faces. Every time we tried to stop, someone would make a funny sound, setting everyone off again.

"Guys, stop!" Amber squeaked out between gasps. "I'm going to pee my pants!"

She got up and waddled toward the bathroom. Her legs were glued together from the knees up, which only made it funnier. Rachel snorted, which got us going all over again.

After a few more minutes of wiping away happy tears, blowing noses, and drinking the rest of their coffee and my tea, we finally started to breathe normally. The breakfast dishes would have to wait on the table as we recovered.

"We should probably clean up," Maya said eventually, still recovering.

We started clearing the table, working together to clean the kitchen. The jazz played softly in the background, and a comfortable, happy energy filled the room.

"It's so great that you can go through so much and still laugh, Rachel," Leah said as she rinsed plates and loaded them in the dishwasher.

"Well, when you go through it, you find out real quick that you're either going to spend your time laughing or crying. I decided early on that I was going to laugh as much as possible."

"Damn, Rachel," I said, "I want to be *you* when I grow up."

"Same," Maya added.

Amber had collected stray water glasses on her way back into the kitchen and started placing them in the dishwasher next to Rachel. "I mean, you never really know how you'd react after getting a diagnosis like that. I can only hope I'd handle it the same way."

Rachel dried her hands on a towel. "Well, like I said last night, sometimes the only way out of something is *through*. I couldn't control much, but I could choose my attitude.

"And I had help along the way from some really good friends." She smiled at all of us. "Thank you for being there. You don't know what those conversations and messages did for me when I was going through the hardest part of it."

"And the wigs!" Maya said. "Was our 'Operation Wiggin' Out' successful?"

"Yes! So many wigs!" Rachel beamed. "They made me smile, and they were a big hit with the students! They looked forward to finding out which wig I would wear that day. One teacher even made little bingo cards for her class—they'd mark off whichever wig I wore each day, and the first one to fill their card won a basket of candy bars. The rainbow wig was everyone's favorite. So many of them took selfies with me on rainbow day."

"We had a blast getting you those wigs," I said. "Do you still wear them?"

"Not as much now that my hair is growing back. They're warm, and, well, hot flashes. So I only wear them when I'm going out. But I do wish my hair was longer."

"Let's get some extensions for you!" Amber said. "I can totally set you up!"

"I'd love that, Amber."

Rachel looked at all of us. "Really, guys, thank you. It's been the fight of my life, and you made it so much more bearable."

"We were honored to be there for you," Leah answered. "Now, let's go walk off that breakfast. The beach is calling our names."

We grabbed our sunglasses and headed for the door, ready to feel the sand between our toes one more time before we had to leave this magical weekend behind.

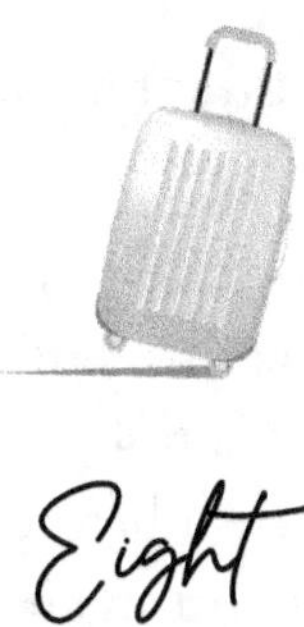

Eight

We stepped out onto the warm, loose sand and instantly fell in step. The sun was bright, but a breeze off the ocean kept it comfortable. I grabbed my little speaker and pulled up my "Chick Chill" playlist. Sade's voice floated quietly around us as we headed toward the green and white umbrellas that lined the edge of the Rosewood Miramar Beach Hotel.

I used the suction cup on the speaker to stick it to my shoulder, so we could all hear the music over the waves. "Say a prayer that this thing doesn't give me a hickey!"

Amber turned and nearly lost her flip-flop. "A hickey?! Oh my gosh, Lisa! I didn't realize that speaker would stick to your skin!"

"Yeah it's pretty classic. Sometimes, when I'm walking around the garden at home, I'll stick it to my forehead, but I'm always afraid it will leave a mark. We won't be out here too long. It should be fine on my shoulder." I pushed it against my skin just a little bit more to make sure it was stuck.

For a while, we didn't say anything. We were soaking it all in—the seagulls crying out to one another as they surfed the wind, the waves rolling in, each one curling and breaking with a foamy rush before sliding back out to sea, and the smell of the salty ocean air filling our lungs.

Amber stretched her arms out wide. "I really needed this weekend with you guys. I didn't realize how wound up I was. I feel like I've decompressed. Thank you for getting together like this. There's nothing quite like old friends."

Decompressed. What a great word. I let my shoulders drop a little. I realized I hadn't truly relaxed and taken a deep breath since Edna died. I closed my eyes and turned into the sun. I focused on the warmth on my face, breathing deep and letting the tension release all the way down to my feet.

We joked and reminisced as we walked along, listening to the waves, watching a few early-morning joggers pass by. The hotel came into full view—a beautiful sprawling property with guests sitting out on their balconies overlooking the beach, reading books, sipping coffee, sunning themselves.

"Hey, whatever happened to Heather Jones?" Maya asked. "Did any of you keep in touch with—"

Suddenly, a faint wisp of cigarette smoke drifted through the air, jolting me out of the peaceful moment.

"Where is that smell coming from?" I asked, looking around.

"What smell?" Leah asked.

"Cigarette smoke. On the beach! Are you kidding me?"

I spotted him—a hotel worker in the traditional black pants and white tuxedo shirt, standing off to the side near the building, smoking a cigarette.

"That jerk," I said, my voice sharper than I intended. "That totally reminds me of Edna. That's exactly what she'd do at this beautiful five-star hotel. She would find an effing spot to go smoke her cigarette."

"Are you okay, Lisa?" Maya asked.

"You've gotta be kidding me." I could feel heat rising in my chest. "I just wanted a weekend free of her. I didn't want to think about her at all. But no, here she is. Not even death is going to get in her way."

I gestured toward the hotel. "Look at that view. This gorgeous hotel on Miramar Beach. And it would be SO like her to ruin it with her inconsiderate cigarette smoking. People are up there on their balconies, trying to enjoy their breakfast and mimosas and their ocean view, paying a fortune for these rooms, and they can smell cigarette smoke because this guy is standing down there smoking, not even caring about who he's affecting. It was so her style."

My words started coming faster now. "She was so selfish with her cigarettes all the time. My clothes always stunk. Even after college, when I lived with her for a short time, I had to buy portable closets and keep all my stuff out in the garage so my clothes didn't smell disgusting. God forbid that woman would go outside to smoke. Her thought process was, 'This is my house. I'm going to do whatever I want to do.'"

I let out a heavy sigh. "Okay, sorry. I'm done talking about her now."

They all looked at each other, silently debating who was going to be the first to say something.

Rachel finally spoke up. "No, you're not done. Lisa, I know you didn't want to talk about Edna at all this weekend, but obviously, you need to because it's spilling out of you. And it's not healthy to keep all that bad stuff in."

"Girl, it's time to unpack that," Amber said. "We're here. Talk to us."

I opened my mouth to object, then closed it again. "I give up," I said, throwing up my hands. I turned and faced the ocean.

"I'm just ... I'm angry at Edna. And I can't *not* be angry."

The waves rolled in, steady and relentless.

"I went to ten different elementary schools because she was never content. We moved all over the place. She was always buying more clothes, more makeup, more things because she wanted to make herself look good. She always wanted a new house because it had to be brand new. She always wanted, wanted, wanted. But it was never enough."

"Oh, I hear you, Lisa," Leah said quietly. Our eyes met. "That's exactly the way my mom was. Never thin enough. Her makeup was never right. Her hair was never perfect. And she was miserable about it. So I understand that."

"Yeah, wasn't your mom kind of hard on you?" Rachel asked.

"Hard enough to make me not want to be around her very much," Leah said. "But that's in the past."

"Edna was kinda hard on me too, but in a different way," I said. "She was passive-aggressive. She expected me to make her happy, to live in her world on her terms. To serve her. My world didn't exist except to try to make her world better."

I could feel the anger building in my chest, tightening like a fist.

"And I tried *so hard* to make her happy. But there was always something wrong. I was never enough."

The words hung in the air. The seagulls squawked overhead, and the waves crashed before me.

"She would call me on the phone in her whiny voice. 'My windows are so dirty.' Of course they were dirty— she was a two-pack-a-day smoker. So what did Lisa do? I hired a window washer and paid for it and had them out immediately so she'd be happy. And then I'd hear, 'Oh, they missed a spot.'"

I could hear her voice in my head. "'My house is so dirty.' She was a cleaning lady, so her house was always very clean. 'My stove—I just can't get my stove clean.' So I'd send a cleaning service. 'Oh, thank you, thank you. But don't send that same one next time. They weren't very good.'"

My voice was rising now.

"I just wanted to scream, 'Can you just be freaking grateful for once?' She manipulated me because she knew I would feel bad. She knew I was a server. She knew I wanted to please. So I would send her whatever she needed, and of course I would pay for it. But instead of being thankful, she always looked for something negative.

"I never felt like I actually succeeded in pleasing her. No matter how hard I tried. I just had to wait for the next demand she had for me, and I was going to fall short on that one, too. That was my life."

"That had to be so hard," Maya said with concern in her voice.

"Yeah, everything had to be clean. Everything had to be folded perfectly and placed properly on tables. We lived in multiple tiny 500-square-foot apartments most of those years, but everything had to be immaculate. She depended on me to keep everything up to her standards. I was the only one who could do it for her, and I was good at it. But even with all of that, it was never enough. She never saw all I did well. She only saw what was less than perfect.

"And I appreciate some of it. I mean, I love that I'm neat and organized and clean. I love that I can make something beautiful. But it also gets in the way. If I'm not careful, it messes with my friendships."

I turned to look at them. "If I stick up for myself, I get accused of being bitchy and needing to have my own way. So I don't stick up for myself very often—and I could never do it with Edna. She'd shoot me down. So there are times when I won't say what I really think because I don't want to be controlling, and I'm afraid of hurting somebody's feelings. I saw Edna hurt people and turn her head and walk away and not even care."

My voice cracked. "And the worst part? I got this fault-finding from Edna, and then I started doing it to my kids. Oh my gosh, both of them are more amazing than I could have hoped for, but I'm always trying to perfect things and make everything better, and it can be too much.

"Kole said the other day, 'I feel like I'm never good enough for your standards. Something always has to be made better. You tell me that something is really great, but ...'

"And Lex ... she keeps many of her feelings to herself, but I can see it in her actions. I hope she doesn't do that to her kids like I did to her.

"I never meant to sound like Edna, but it's still with me. It's definitely where I got it wrong as a mom."

The tears were coming now.

"Damn it! I'm in my fifties, and I still struggle with hearing her in my head. Sometimes I find myself really angry because I want to be me, but I hear Edna in my head telling me to be something that she wants me to be. And I'm not afforded the opportunity to just ... be. Not because somebody's holding it back from me. I'm holding it back from myself. And I really blame Edna for that. And that makes me angry."

I wiped away my tears with the back of my hand.

"When do I get to just *be* without performing for someone?"

The weight of it all pressed down on me.

"I can't find a single happy memory with her. Not one. For good or for bad, I'm telling you, I can't find a thought in my head where I'm like, 'Oh, that was a really fun time with Mom.' I can remember back to when I was three years old, but I still can't find a memory where I was like, 'I love that she was my mom.' I have a hard time being grateful. And it sucks because I'm a very, very grateful person. But with my mom, I can't find it."

I took a shaky breath.

"I mean, I'm grateful for who I am. I like who I am. She needed to be in my life to shape who I am now. But ..."

I stopped. The hardest truth sat on my tongue.

"I was relieved when she died."

There. I'd said it. Rachel reached out and touched my arm, encouraging me to keep going.

"I know it sounds crazy and super raw and not very kind, but I'm telling you, I'm so thankful I don't have to deal with that anymore. The judging, the manipulation, the whining, the complaining, the bitterness, the talking behind people's backs. All of it. I loved my mom, but it was hard. And I'm just ... I'm so mad."

Rachel stepped closer. "You know what you need to do? You need to let it *out*. Really let it out."

I looked at her, then at the ocean.

Before I could talk myself out of it, I turned and walked straight into the water. The waves broke around my ankles—shocking, cold. But I felt something release in me.

I gathered every ounce of anger I had and started yelling.

"YOU WERE NEVER CONTENT WITH ANYTHING!"

The wave whooshed in, pulling at my feet.

"NOTHING I DID WAS EVER GOOD ENOUGH!"

The wind whipped my hair.

"I ALWAYS GAVE YOU ALL THE THINGS YOU NEEDED IN LIFE!"

The sand shifted beneath me.

"I TRIED SO HARD! WHY COULDN'T YOU BE GRATEFUL? EVEN ONCE? IT WAS NEVER, EVER ENOUGH!"

My voice broke.

"WHEN DO I GET TO LIVE MY LIFE? WHEN DO I GET TO JUST BE ME?"

The ocean roared back. The receding water seemed to be pulling my anger out of me.

"YOU DON'T GET TO CONTROL AND MANIPULATE ME ANYMORE! YOU CAN'T JUDGE MY EFFORTS ANYMORE! I'M DONE!"

I stood there, tears streaming down my face, waves washing over my feet and pulling the sand out from under me. Everything—all the anger, all the hurt, all the trying—sliding away with the sand.

For a moment, the pounding inside my head drowned out all other noise.

Then I heard Maya's gentle voice: "How did that feel?"

I turned to look at them, still standing on dry sand, watching me.

I pulled myself together. And then, to everyone's surprise, I started to laugh.

"Actually ... that felt really, really good." I wiped my face. "You guys should try it."

Amber stepped forward, hesitated for just a second, then walked into the water beside me. The cold water made her gasp. Then she let out a giggle. "I guess I'm game."

Rachel started stepping forward as Amber faced the ocean and yelled: "I MADE A MISTAKE! THAT'S ALL! I'M DONE BEING ASHAMED!"

The wave rushed in, washing around her ankles. I let out a whoop and said, "You go, girl!"

Rachel was next. She walked in on my other side, rolled her shoulders back, and shouted: "FUCK YOU, CANCER! YOU DON'T GET TO WIN! YOU DON'T GET TO RUIN MY LIFE ANYMORE!"

We all cheered.

"That's right, Rachel! Cancer can't have you!" Amber shouted.

Maya stepped forward, then looked back at Leah, smiling. She hooked her arm into Leah's. "Come on, Leah. Time to let go and live a little."

Leah hesitated, glancing around at the beach, at the hotel, clearly worried about who might be watching. Then she looked at Maya and walked into the surf with her.

She stood there for a moment, then cupped her hands around her mouth and yelled: "I'M ENOUGH! I'M ENOUGH JUST AS I AM! AND I AM LOVED!"

More hollering. More cheers. This felt really, really good.

Maya grinned and stepped in beside her. "SCREW YOU, MARK! MY LIFE IS GOING TO BE SO MUCH BETTER WITHOUT YOU! I CAN'T WAIT FOR THE REST OF MY LIFE TO HAPPEN! YOU CAN HAVE YOUR LITTLE MUFFIN, I'VE GOT THE ENTIRE BAKERY!"

"Whooo hooo!" Amber shouted in delight. "Come on, Maya! Tell it!"

We stood there together, the five of us in a line, conquerors. The waves washed up around our feet and ankles, pulling on us. All the stuff we'd been carrying for so long—all that heavy, painful stuff—sliding out of us like the sand slipping away beneath our feet.

From my shoulder, "Royals" by Lorde started to play. I started singing along, snapping my fingers and swaying side to side. The others joined me. Soon we were all dancing, splashing, the water spraying up a fine mist around us. We laughed as the receding waves tried to pull us off balance, grabbing onto each other to stay upright.

We felt so free. So happy. For a minute, it felt like it was just us on the beach, and nothing else mattered.

When the song ended, we turned and walked out of the surf, our shorts wet, our feet covered in sand.

I looked up at the hotel.

Now it wasn't just the guy smoking. Several other hotel workers had joined him, and they were all standing there, staring at us. One guy had his phone out, clearly recording.

"Oops," I said.

Rachel shrugged. "Well, we gave them some great content."

Leah cupped her hands around her mouth and yelled up to them, "Hope you enjoyed the show!"

We all stopped and stared at her.

"Who are you and what have you done with Leah?" Rachel asked.

I turned away to hide my smile, and out of the corner of my eye, I caught Leah smiling at Maya. Maya winked back.

"Why do I feel like we just got put on some sort of list?" Rachel said with a laugh. "I don't think we'll ever be able to set foot in that hotel."

Leah shook out her hair before pulling it back into a low ponytail. "Oh, I'd do it all over again."

"Me too," I said. "I really do feel better."

Rachel turned to me with a concerned look. "Lisa, don't ever say that you're bitchy or controlling ever again. You are a leader, and you lead with excellence in all you do. Leaders aren't always everyone's cup of tea, but that's okay. You're organized and get shit done. More than most people."

There was a chorus of agreement from the others.

I looked down at the sand, letting that sink in. I teared up a little. "Thank you. And, if I haven't said it enough, I'm so grateful to have you guys in my life."

We started walking back along the beach, our wet feet coated in sand. The conversation was light and easy now—talking about the people and things waiting for us when we got home, what we were going to tell our families about this trip, what we were going to remember most.

After a few minutes, I stopped and turned to face them.

"You guys, thank you for letting me vent. You took the time to hear me. Let me feel without judging. And you don't think I'm crazy." I paused. "Or maybe you're as crazy as I am, and that feels good too."

"We're definitely as crazy as you are," Amber said.

"And it's just different when we're all together in person. I couldn't have said those things over the phone. It's more powerful having you here, getting in my face a little."

"I feel the same way," said Amber. "I needed this face-to-face time, but I didn't know I needed it."

As we walked, Rachel was starting to look a little tired from all the exercise and the emotional weight of the morning.

Maya noticed. "How are you feeling, Rachel?"

"My energy runs out pretty quickly these days. But I'm happy."

Amber said, "We should probably head back and get cleaned up and packed. We've got to check out soon."

"Yeah," Leah said. "And I'm going to have to start all over with my hair and makeup."

"Was it worth it?" I asked with a grin.

"Totally worth it," Leah said, her face beaming.

Amber studied her. "You're different today, you know that?"

Leah looked at Maya with a knowing grin. "I'm learning how to let go a little."

We turned and headed back to the Airbnb, leaving our footprints in the sand behind us.

Nine

We showered and did our hair and makeup, then stripped the beds and finished everything on the checkout list. We piled our luggage into the back of the Jeep one last time and jumped in. It was a much tighter fit this time because I added my kitchen shipment to the mix.

"Shotgun!" Maya called as she headed for the front seat.

As we pulled away, Amber waved at the Airbnb. "Bye, house! It was fun while it lasted!"

We all laughed as we waved along with her.

Our first stop was the UPS Store to mail off my box of items that I had sent from home. Then we headed back to the airport, listening to the "Santa Barbara Babes" playlist one last time together. We were belting out Tom Petty's "Free Falling" as we merged onto the 101.

As we sang and joked, the wind blowing through our hair, the sun shining down on us, we slipped back into the easy, familiar rhythm from long ago. All the barriers were gone. We had settled back into our old ways. We were just best friends from high school again. We had reconnected so much that it seemed to erase the years.

I glanced over at Maya, then in my rearview mirror at the girls in the back seat, and something magical happened.

For just a moment, we weren't a group of women in our fifties. Riding in that Jeep, we were suddenly seventeen again—boy crazy, not sure what our futures would hold, but certain that whatever happened, we'd face it together. We were an army of five. Us against the world. I didn't want to even blink.

I felt a surge of gratitude as I turned my attention back to the road. I had put together this trip as a gift to them, but they were actually the gift back to me.

We dropped our Jeep off at the rental car return and started lugging our baggage into the airport. The doors whooshed open, and we were hit with the smell of Mexican food and margaritas.

I inhaled deeply. "This is the best-smelling airport in the world!"

Rachel laughed. "Well, let's check our bags and get through security, and then maybe we can get some of that yummy food."

Twenty minutes later, we walked into the Costa Terraza Restaurant with our small carry-ons. We had just enough time for some appetizers and margaritas. Even Amber ordered a virgin margarita.

"Oh look," said Maya, "we're eating food that you didn't have to cook."

"It's not as good as my cooking, that's for sure!" I said jokingly.

"True. But really, I would love to help with the food next time," said Maya.

"We'd all like to help next time. You've shown us how it's done," said Leah.

I got an idea. "Hey, why don't you guys send me some of your favorite recipes, and I'll put them together in a cookbook and call it something like *The Girlfriend's Gathering Table.* Then we'll cook from those recipes next time."

"That sounds great!" said Leah. "It will be interesting to see what kind of food we come up with. It will be … eclectic, I'm sure."

After we ate, I opened up my carry-on. "Before we go our separate ways, I have one more gift I want to give you guys. Something that will make you think about our time together."

"You've got to be kidding, Lisa," Rachel said. "You've already given us so much."

I began handing out four small boxes. "I saw these when I found the coffee mugs, and they're just too cool not to have. I love to find things that make a trip special. I revel in all the little details that let you know how important you are to me."

"You're like Julie from *The Love Boat*," Rachel said as they all opened their boxes. "You could totally do this kind of stuff for a living."

"Oh wow!" Leah said as she picked up the dainty metal bracelet. It had a beautiful silver charm with a wave on it. "You're right, this is so cool!"

"I think we need to keep having these get-togethers at different destinations," I said. "With every girls' weekend we have, we can add a charm to represent where we stay. I was just thinking about the beach when I bought them, but the wave seems more fitting now than ever, since the waves are where we left all of our baggage!"

"I *love* that, Lisa," Amber said. We watched her as she studied the bracelet. Her eyes started to tear up. I could tell she was trying to gather her thoughts.

"You know, I was really looking forward to this trip because I love you guys, and it was going to be so fun to hang out again, but ... it turned out to be so much more than anything I had expected."

Her voice caught. "This weekend changed my life. I came here feeling so heavy, but I don't think I even recognized that. I was so ashamed of the drinking. I was just getting through each day. But you guys listened to me and loved on me even after finding out, and this huge load got lifted off me. The more we all talked, the lighter I felt."

She wiped a tear away. "I need you guys. I need this. It's great that we text and use Marco Polo. I love looking at your social media posts. But ... this is something different—"

"Aww, Amber, we need you too," I said. "And I agree—those conversations have changed me. Never in a million years did I think I would be yelling at the top of my lungs into the ocean, but I did it, and I feel so much better now."

Leah looked at her carry-on bag sitting beside the table. "Man, we came with a lot more baggage than we thought! Good thing the airlines don't charge extra for emotional baggage, or we'd all be broke."

"Ain't that the truth!" said Rachel.

"Seriously though," Leah continued, "I'm glad we're leaving some of that crap behind."

We laughed and chatted until it was time to pay the check and get to the gates. Everyone was flying out at close to the same time, except me—I was flying out a little later that day. I like being the first one in and the last one out.

We paid the check and walked together toward the gates, our small bags in hand.

"Maya, text me when you start looking at bakery locations," I said. "Maybe I can fly out there and help you look."

"Deal," Maya said, squeezing my arm.

"And Amber," Rachel said, "don't forget about those extensions. I'm serious."

"I've already got ideas," Amber grinned.

Rachel was the first to peel off toward her gate. We all hugged her tight.

"Love you guys," she said, her voice catching. "This weekend ... thank you."

Maya and Leah were on the same flight, so they headed off together in the opposite direction, waving over their shoulders.

Amber hugged me one last time. "Keep your chin up, Amber," I said. "You're going to be okay. Better than okay."

She grinned. "Thanks, Lisa. Your support means everything to me." She slung her small bag over her shoulder and turned to walk away.

I stood there for a moment, watching my friends disappear into the airport crowd, each heading to their own gate, their own life, their own home.

But something had shifted. We weren't the same people who'd arrived here three days ago.

I bought a bottle of water and a journal at the bookstore, then headed to my gate, even though it would be another two hours before I could board. I had so many thoughts swirling through my head, and I just wanted to write, to process.

I found a seat near the window and opened the journal to the first page.

Amber's words kept echoing in my mind. *This weekend changed my life. I came here feeling so heavy ... but you guys listened to me and loved on me ... and this huge load got lifted off me.*

That's what had happened to all of us, wasn't it? We'd all come carrying something. And somehow, by the end of this weekend, our loads felt lighter.

I thought about the beach this morning. About yelling into the ocean. About Rachel cursing at cancer. About Leah declaring she was enough. About Maya claiming her future and Amber releasing her shame.

Our suitcases were actually heavier when we left with all of our shopping and souvenirs. But the baggage we'd been carrying long before we packed for this trip got left behind.

I started writing, and suddenly I was back in my childhood.

Every morning when I was growing up, I would wake up to the same scene. Edna sitting at the kitchen countertop in her robe in whatever apartment, trailer, or duplex we were living in at the time.

> Every single morning, without fail, she'd be in her spot. Always a bar stool or chair right next to the phone. She would smoke her cigarette, drink her first cup of coffee, and catch up with her friends.
>
> "Hi, Patti, what are you doing today? This is what I'm doing today ..." The conversation was always predictable. "All right, I gotta go. I'll talk to you later."
>
> Then she'd call Hair Pat—we called her that because she did my mom's hair. Same exact format. "Hi, what are you doing today? Here's all the gossip. I'll talk to you later."
>
> She'd go through a couple of these conversations, then finish her cigarette, do the dishes, and go get ready for work.

I paused, staring at what I'd written.

Those morning phone calls were Edna's lifeline. Her version of connection. Gossip and complaints and "what are you doing today"—that was her girlfriendship.

But what we'd done this weekend was different. Deeper. More real.

I kept writing.

> I became an overachiever, a people-pleaser of sorts because of Edna. She always said, "Lisa can do it.

Lisa's good at it. Look how cute Lisa is. Give it to Lisa, she can fix it." And I learned. I learned to figure out what she needed and how to give it to her.

But underneath all of that was fear.

Edna discarded people. My half-sister, when she didn't do what Edna wanted. My dad. Houses that didn't please her. I learned early: if you don't please Edna, you're gone.

So I learned how to serve and please. So I would never be discarded.

I set down my pen and took a drink of water.

That's what I'd been doing my whole life, wasn't it? Performing. Serving. Making everything beautiful and perfect so people wouldn't leave.

But this weekend, my friends had seen me at my worst—angry, raw, yelling into the ocean about my dead mother—and they hadn't left. They'd walked into the water with me.

I looked around the airport. People everywhere, heads down, staring at phones. Thumbs scrolling. Faces glowing blue.

I picked up my pen again.

We've lost something as a society. We're surrounded by technology—TV, phones, computers, social media. We have friends on speed dial, the world at our fingertips. And yet we're more emotionally isolated than we've ever been.

Social media gives us touchpoints. Likes and heart emojis and quick comments. But when it really matters, likes won't help us. There's so much more to friendship than we realize, and we're sacrificing it to busyness and settling for those hollow little interactions.

What we did this weekend was different. Face-to-face. Looking each other in the eye. Sitting with each other when it didn't feel good. That's the solid foundation we've lost.

And that's what I needed. That's what we all needed.

You can tell me something in a text or an email. But it's not until I'm with you one-on-one, where you actually say to me, "Lisa, wake up. Give yourself a little grace"—that's when it lands. That's when things change.

I glanced down at my carry-on bag sitting at my feet.

And suddenly, it clicked.

BAGS.

Not just the physical luggage we'd hauled through the airport. The emotional baggage we'd all been carrying.

Here's what I learned this weekend: when you name it, you start loosening its grip. And when you share it with the right people—your girlfriends, your safe people—you start lightening your load.

Just like a physical piece of baggage, it's not actually part of who you are. You can set it down. You can walk away from it.

I thought about Amber's guilt. About Leah's perfectionism. About Rachel's cancer. About Maya's divorce. About my years of overachieving for approval.

That invisible baggage was heavy, exhausting, and isolating.

But we'd set some of our bags down this weekend.

That's when it hit me. Our bags were weighing us down. All of a sudden, I realized I had an acronym for what we had built together:

B—Bonding

A—Awareness

G—Guidance

S—Sisterhood

And I knew beyond a doubt that I needed to share our story and this framework with other women.

Because how many women out there are carrying baggage and never letting it go? How many are isolated, performing, afraid to be real because they might be discarded?

What if we could give them permission to set it down? To find their people and unpack?

I looked out the window at the planes taking off and landing. People going home. People starting new journeys.

I closed my journal and thought about it all.

I thought about my childhood. The moving, the constant reinventing, always trying to please people to get praise. I thought about Edna and how complicated our relationship was. The cigarettes and her daily phone calls to catch the latest gossip. How she was always searching for something but never seemed to find it.

I thought about her waiting for me to get to her bedside. About her taking her last breath.

I wasn't Edna's doll anymore. I wasn't performing for her approval. I didn't have to be perfect to avoid being discarded.

I could just be Lisa. Imperfect, messy, sometimes angry, sometimes too-controlling Lisa. And my friends loved me anyway.

The loudspeaker crackled: "Now boarding Flight 1247 to Minneapolis."

I gathered my things and stood up, slinging my bag over my shoulder.

I finally understood.

Edna is gone. She's finally free from it all.

And so am I.

Epilogue

Connecting virtually can trick us into thinking we're closer than we are. You can follow someone's life for years—know what they ordered for brunch, where they vacationed, what made them laugh that week—and still not know what they're actually carrying.

The deeper stuff doesn't come out over a text. It comes out when you're sharing space, when there's nowhere else to be, when the conversation finally gets quiet enough to go somewhere real. That kind of friendship takes practice. You have to show up for it.

It wasn't until I was sitting at my gate that afternoon with a brand-new journal and two hours to kill that I started making these connections. I didn't realize I was writing the first page of something much bigger than a journal entry. Much bigger than even a book.

The BAGS framework came to me in a rush. It was one of those rare moments where something you've lived finally organizes itself into words. I wrote until my hand cramped.

What I couldn't see then was where it would lead.

In the months after Santa Barbara, I found myself thinking about that weekend constantly—not just our specific conversations, but the shape of what had happened to us. Five women who thought they were taking a vacation and accidentally gave each other something they didn't know they needed: a safe place to finally set it all down.

I started talking about it. To friends. To women I barely knew. In grocery stores, on planes, and at dinner tables. Long phone calls that started as check-ins and became confessions. And what I kept hearing, over and over, was some version of the same thing: *I've been carrying this for years, but I've never told anyone.*

That sentence broke my heart. And every time, it made me more certain that what happened in Santa Barbara wasn't a fluke. It was a framework. So I built something around it.

That's how my brand, You Go Girl, was born—out of one weekend trip that changed the lives of five women who thought they were just going to the beach.

We thought we were there to laugh, eat good food, and catch up on the years we'd let slip by. What we discovered instead was that every single one of us was carrying something we'd never said out loud. And the moment we finally did, everything got a little lighter.

I couldn't stop thinking about how many other women were out there doing exactly what we'd been doing for years:

hauling it all alone, holding it together, pretending the load wasn't heavy. So I built a place for them, too.

You Go Girl is a community for women who are ready to stop carrying it all by themselves. Through the BAGS framework, this book, a cookbook, a podcast, a speaking tour, travel guides for planning your own girls' trips, and a curated product line, everything I am creating is designed to do one thing: spark the kind of authentic connection that actually changes you.

From the pages we read together to the tables we gather around to the adventures I'll inspire you to take, this is a place that honors the quiet, often-overlooked power of girlfriendship. Not the curated kind. The real kind. The kind that shows up when things get messy, that listens without fixing, that says *I see what you're carrying* and doesn't flinch.

There's plenty of laughter, too. But at the center of it all is the belief that every woman deserves someone in her corner who simply gets her.

That's You Go Girl. And you're exactly who it was made for.

Before we dive into the framework, I have a question for you.

What are you carrying right now that no one else knows about?

Not your purse or your to-do list or the mental load of what's for dinner tonight. The invisible weight. The thing you've been hauling around for months, maybe years. The secret. The shame. The guilt. The grief. The anger you've never fully expressed. The dream you gave up. The words you wish you'd said—or the ones you can never take back.

We all carry it. Every single one of us. And we've gotten so good at pretending the load isn't heavy that we've forgotten we're even carrying it.

Girl, it's time to unpack that baggage.

The BAGS Framework

Most women don't talk about the invisible challenges they face. The abuse they suffer. The health issues they navigate. The loss of identity or career or loved ones. When life takes a turn that no one planned for, we tend to struggle in silence.

We put on a smile, we stay strong, and we take care of everyone else around us.

But baggage doesn't disappear just because we carry it well. Instead, it gets heavier.

That weekend with my girlfriends stayed with me long after it ended. Something shifted when we finally let ourselves be honest—really honest—and I walked away feeling lighter than I had in years.

As I processed it all through journaling, a pattern started to emerge. We didn't realize it then, but we had experienced something magical that, with some intention, could be repeated. I called it the BAGS Framework, which stands for Bonding, Awareness, Guidance, and Sisterhood. And I knew I had to share it.

Bonding starts with feeling like we're in a safe space. Before we can share what we're carrying, we have to feel that level of comfort to set it down. That means finding those friends who don't judge us, who don't pull away when things get messy. It's the laughter that comes before the deep conversations. Trust builds slowly, over time, until one day we realize we don't have to hold that heavy weight on our own. That's what turns friendship into the kind of girlfriendship where we truly see each other in an unconditional light.

Awareness is when we finally tell ourselves the truth about what we have been carrying in silence. Not the version we show everyone else, but the real one. The exhaustion. The loneliness we struggle to explain. The slow, quiet realization that something in our life no longer fits who we're becoming. That's when the baggage finally begins to unzip.

Guidance means walking alongside one another without trying to fix anything. When we lift each other up rather than call each other out, we are reminded of who we really are. Most problems don't have easy answers, but having a trusted friend who listens without judgment can help us work through even the hardest things we carry.

Sisterhood keeps those bags from ever getting too heavy again. Women aren't meant to carry their burdens alone. We need ongoing conversations with shared laughter and tears, reminding us that support doesn't end when the hard stuff begins. Women who unpack invisible baggage together create a safety net for other women to do the same.

Want the Full BAGS Guide?

What you've just read is only the beginning.

Inside the **You Go Girl Sisterhood**, members will receive the full BAGS framework including:

- A "How-To" process for unpacking conversations
- Girlfriendship discussion prompts
- Steps to enter the Sisterhood Circle
- Travel accessories and guides to facilitate your weekend away with friends
- Live Zooms within the Sisterhood Circle to unpack with support

If *Girl, Unpack That!* spoke to you, it might be because you already know something many women ultimately discover:

Life is lighter when we unpack it together.

Join the sisterhood and receive the complete BAGS framework and more at:

You-Go-Girl.com

Book Club Discussion Guide

Girl, Unpack That

1. The women in this story gather to tell the truth about what they've been carrying. Why do you think women often wait for a specific setting (a trip, a crisis, a milestone) before they allow themselves to open up?

2. How has the role of "the strong one" shaped the way you move through your friendships? Has strength ever kept you from being fully known?

3. This book suggests that sisterhood requires intention, not just proximity. Do you agree? What distinguishes true sisterhood from simply having friends?

4. Many women carry silent narratives about who they are supposed to be. What expectations (cultural, familial, or self-imposed) have most influenced your relationships with other women?

5. Was there a moment in the book where you felt uncomfortable or challenged? Why do you think that moment landed the way it did?

6. How do women unintentionally compete with one another, even when they genuinely want connection?

7. The idea of "unpacking" implies both honesty and vulnerability. What do you think prevents women from doing that more often?

8. The BAGS concept in the book speaks to bonding, awareness, guidance, and sisterhood as stages of connection. Which stage do you believe most women skip—and what is lost when they do?

As you close this chapter of reflection, my hope is that you have been able to unpack some of your baggage in the safe space among your friends.

Your journey will ultimately be what you make of it, shaped by the effort and intention you bring to unpacking your own story, just as I have done through the years.

My journey has been filled with many friends who have walked alongside me—many women and some men. I would like to pause and recognize them for their impact on my life.

Acknowledgments

This book would never have found its arms and legs without the people I gathered around me, those who listened as the words found their way to the page, stood watch like armor when I felt exposed, and cradled me with gentleness when I needed to be held. So many of you have taken hours out of your life to support me in many ways, and it has not gone unnoticed. To each of you, my deepest gratitude.

It feels appropriate to first acknowledge the three women who were the inspiration (although we didn't know it at the time) for this book: my dear friends since the age of twelve, **Cindy, Michelle,** and **Sandy.** A girls' trip we took together years ago planted a seed and opened the door to conversations that stayed with me long after we returned home and immediately had me creating the story you now hold in your hands.

While the friendships that inspired this book are very real in my life, the women and stories within these pages are works of fiction, shaped from the kind of experiences, emotions, and conversations so many women carry. The characters were very intentionally created to resonate with women everywhere, not to tell the literal stories of my friends I cherish so deeply.

Without our decades of friendship, the funny and the sad, the tears of laughter and those of pain, the arguments and reconciliations, I may never have found the determination to express myself in this way or to encourage other women to do the same.

It is rare in life to be blessed with friendships like the ones I share with you three that have endured over time. When I think of how we've matured over time, individually, together, apart, and together again, through childhood, partying through high school, the wild days of young adulthood, motherhood, marriage, divorce, and now menopause, I am reminded just how incredible it is to still be walking through life with you.

To share a friendship that has lasted so many seasons of life is a gift I will never take for granted. I am deeply grateful to be walking life's journey with you, and I look forward to many more chapters together. Love you all! XO

Pete: You are the strength in my life that keeps me grounded and lifts me above the clouds. Thank you for letting me step away from being a wife for a little while to spend countless hours reflecting, reminiscing, and writing these words over and over again. It felt never-ending, but you hung in there and believed in me when I needed it most. Your immeasurable support for me is undeniably one of the most comforting aspects of my life. What we share is genuine and deep, the kind of connection that only comes from something truly real. It cannot be purchased online, can't be borrowed, and certainly can't be faked. Thanks for stickin' around … I'm the luckiest girl in the world. I love you! XO

Doodle: My tech-savvy daughter! Talk about patience. Thank you, Lex, for the countless hours you spend hearing me ask the same things over and over again: "How do I get that link? Where do I find … ? I lost my words, how do I get them back?" All of it, Lex! I appreciate you always being there to help with the computer stuff and the endurance you always seem to have for your crazy mom. Your undying loyalty to me, even when we don't agree, is unmatched. Thank you for your grace. Fitting for this book, we, too, share a friendship that runs deep. My hope is that it will be passed down to your daughter as well. It's a true gift that many don't get to experience. We are blessed. I love you! XO

Kole: Thank you for strategically pointing out that many of my words have resembled those of your grandmother. You are careful in the way you have presented that to me, and I am grateful that you still love me anyway. The last thing in life that I want for my children is to make them feel as though they're not enough. You are enough! It's a continuing struggle to step out of my paradigm, but you are there to keep me in line. Thank you for your support and honesty! I love you! XO

Kathy: From our weekly Zoom calls, to pulling from the original manuscript, to laughing so hard we nearly peed over the realities of what we women face in life, you have been incredible through it all. I am deeply grateful for your guidance in structure and your undying writing support. You beautifully managed to take my sandpaper words and turn them into velvet. Every thought, every word, every story I shared with you came back sounding exactly the way I hoped it would. That is a rare gift. XO, Thank you!

Lori: The behind-the-scenes, most loving, incredibly meticulous editor I have ever had the privilege to work with. The countless hours that you and Kathy took editing and checking and redoing makes my head spin when I actually sit down and process it. I have such deep respect and appreciation for the care that you have taken to help make my work become a perfect piece of art to present to the world. Thank you, truly, for just being you. You are an amazing gem and a light that shines so brightly. XO, Thank you!

Shanda: From our first Zoom, what an amazing opportunity I have been given to work with you. Work ethic is one of the qualities I admire most in people, and you are the queen of it. You get shit done, and it shows! I will never forget the first email you sent back to me. Your words were so heartfelt that I printed the message and placed it in a pink bedazzled frame. Kinda like the first dollar that a business receives from their first sale. Your praise and encouragement meant that much to me. Thank you for your support, your excellence, and the care you bring to everything you do. It has meant more than you might realize. XO!

Leslie: Thanks for batting clean-up! Your trained eye that caught the little things we had seen over and over again gave me great confidence. Thank you. XO

Wootie: You taught me how to write. You helped me omit the clichés, taught me how to use serial commas, and rephrased my sentences until they sounded just right. Most of all, you tolerated my quirks and endless edits. Even though this book is a different version of what you and I started with in 2019, I still couldn't have created the final product without you helping me start it. Thank you! XO

Alex: My new, incredibly supportive friend! Without you, I would have never been able to walk down this beautiful path with such amazing women. Thank you for connecting me with Kathy, Lori, Amanda, and Shanda. Because of you, I found the most incredible women who helped shape this book into what it is today. You're the best. XO

A to the Z! Anthony E. Zuiker: To think you have created so many shows that depict the crazies in this world and then you end up helping a simple girl like me. What a testament to your versatility. When I needed a name for the brand, you came up with *You Go Girl* in just seconds after just a short description in text. Thank you, my dear friend, for your vision, brilliant mind, and kind heart, for always working with me when I need you. I'm forever in your debt. XO

Maria: Te has convertido en mi brazo derecho. He llegado a quererte profundamente y estoy increíblemente agradecida de que formes parte de este mundo de You Go Girl. Lo que empezó como "solo" gestión de redes sociales se ha convertido en algo mucho más. Te has convertido en alguien en quien confío de maneras que nunca imaginé, y eres realmente irremplazable. Esta conexión me ha recordado que cuando tratas a las personas con auténtico amor, cariño y respeto, nunca pasa desapercibido. Tu forma de actuar, tu dedicación y el corazón que pones en todo lo que haces significan más para mí de lo que puedo expresar con palabras. Gracias por todo lo que haces, Mija. Te aprecio más de lo que crees. XO

Amanda: You served as an eye-opening, badass, get-it-done experience with a whole new vocabulary of funnels and cash flow and all the concepts that I didn't know … yet. Your gracious heart allowed me to expand and inspired me to never give up. Thank you. XO

To my Zesties: Katelyn, Lex, and Ben, you started me out on a path that I will always be grateful for. Thank you for your interest and love thrown my way for You Go Girl. XO

To the many friends and family who read bits and pieces of this book: Thank you for reading and rereading to share your thoughts on grammar, typos, and content.

"It takes a village" is my favorite cliché here, and I'm truly grateful for each of you who generously gave your time to help me. XO

To those friends who were once part of my life: I hold a place in my heart for all of the great times that we shared. You taught me something incredibly important … that sometimes letting go is not a failure, but simply a part of life. That understanding has become a meaningful part of my journey with You Go Girl and part of the heart behind this book. I wish you well and thank you for being part of my story. XO

And finally, to you, the reader, my new friend: I hope you find a sense of belonging within these pages. I truly believe our stories are connected in a beautiful, almost intuitive sense, intertwined by shared emotions and lived experiences. I hold that sisterhood connection close; I feel it deeply, whether we're near or far. Thank you for spending time with me through the carefully shaped words on these pages. I hope they resonate with you and offer inspiration, just as you continually inspire me.

About the Author

Lisa **Najarian** is the founder of You Go Girl, a women's platform built on one simple belief: ***life gets lighter when we stop carrying everything alone.***

Known for her warmth, honesty, and ability to make people feel instantly at ease, Lisa creates spaces where women can slow down, tell the truth, and feel a deep sense of belonging.

Much of Lisa's life was spent as what she calls "the perpetual new girl," moving from place to place and learning early how powerful (and complicated) friendship can be. Those experiences shaped her lifelong curiosity about how women connect, how we carry emotional baggage, and how much healing can happen when we unpack it together.

Through her writing, speaking, and her proprietary BAGS framework, Lisa gently guides women to notice what they're holding onto and to set it down in the safe space of girlfriends. Her work isn't about fixing yourself or becoming someone new. It's about living lighter through connection, reflection, and sisterhood.

When she's not writing or gathering women together, Lisa can usually be found cooking in her kitchen, shopping for cute shoes (usually in pink), spending time with her kids and grandkids, or deep in conversation with girlfriends, exactly where she believes the best stories, and the deepest belonging, begin.

An Invitation

Did something in these pages feel familiar? Did you find yourself nodding along, exhaling, or recognizing pieces of your own story? If so, you're not alone. This book is only the beginning of a conversation meant to be shared.

You Go Girl started as one weekend trip that changed the lives of five women who thought they were just going to the beach. Now it's a movement of women who are ready to stop hauling it all alone. It's a community for continued reflection, honest conversation, and learning how to unpack what life asks us to carry … together.

If you've felt a sense of belonging here, consider stepping a little closer. You're invited to continue the journey, deepen the connection, and see what it feels like to be part of something quietly growing and deeply supportive.

Come as you are. Bring whatever you're carrying. We'll unpack it together.

Here's what's waiting for you inside the You Go Girl Sisterhood:

- A **You Go Girl Signature Charm Bracelet**—a reminder that you don't have to carry your baggage alone

- **Travel guides, blogs, and Airbnb recipes** made just for members

- A **Weekly Girlfriend Drop** email packed with inspiration, tips, and fun challenges

- A **Private Sisterhood Group** plus monthly giveaways

- **Printable trip planners, affirmations, and playlists** to use anytime

- **Early access and member discounts** on products and retreats

- **Monthly Carry-On Conversations** with Lisa and special guests

- … **and so much more**

Get access to all of this and more by going to:

You-Go-Girl.com

www.ingramcontent.com/pod-product-compliance
Lightning Source LLC
Chambersburg PA
CBHW071513140726
47997CB00005B/1959